Contents

Unit 1

Unit 2

Unit 3

Week 1: **Number – Number and place value**
Lesson 1, Extension: Scarf patterns
Lesson 2, Support: Flower garden 5s
Lesson 3, Support: Table tennis 10s
Lesson 4, Extension: Pathway patterns

Week 2: **Number – Multiplication and division**
Lesson 1, Support: How many socks?
Lesson 2, Extension: Sticker sets
Lesson 3, Support: Toffee 10s
Lesson 4, Extension: Sheep sharing

Week 3: Geometry – **Position and direction**
Lesson 1, Support: Beach directions
Lesson 2, Support: Where is it?
Lesson 3, Extension: Whole and half turns
Lesson 4, Extension: Quarter and three-quarter turns

Unit 4

Week 1: **Number – Addition and subtraction**
Lesson 1, Extension: How many monkeys?
Lesson 2, Extension: Spider subtraction
Lesson 3, Support: Missing number muddle
Lesson 4, Extension: How many are there?

Week 2: **Number – Fractions**
Lesson 1, Extension: Fruit fractions
Lesson 2, Support: Honeybee halves
Lesson 3, Support: Cube tower halves
Lesson 4, Extension: Half measures

Week 3: **Measurement (money)**
Lesson 1, Extension: Going shopping
Lesson 2, Support: Same amounts
Lesson 3, Extension: Coins and notes
Lesson 4, Support: Money problems

Unit 5

Week 1: **Number – Number and place value**
    Lesson 1, Extension: Ordering owls
    Lesson 2, Support: Odds and evens gardens
    Lesson 3, Support: Wallpaper patterns
    Lesson 4, Extension: Pathway patterns

Week 2: **Number – Addition and subtraction**
    Lesson 1, Support: Coin collections
    Lesson 2, Extension: Making money
    Lesson 3, Extension: What can I buy?
    Lesson 4, Support: How much left?

Week 3: **Geometry – Properties of shape**
    Lesson 1, Extension: Who has which shape?
    Lesson 1, Support: 3-D shape models
    Lesson 2, Extension: 3-D shapes and 2-D shapes
    Lesson 4, Support: 2-D and 3-D shapes

Unit 6

Week 1: **Number – Multiplication and division, including Number and place value**
    Lesson 1, Support: Bug trail 2s
    Lesson 2, Extension: Pattern of 5s
    Lesson 3, Extension: Tomato ketchup 10s
    Lesson 4, Support: All at sea

Week 2: **Number – Multiplication and division**
    Lesson 1, Support: How many bugs?
    Lesson 2, Extension: Shopping problems
    Lesson 3, Support: Sharing spots
    Lesson 4, Extension: Share with friends

Week 3: **Measurement (mass)**
    Lesson 1, Extension: Lightest to heaviest
    Lesson 2, Extension: Comparing mass
    Lesson 3, Support: How many to balance?
    Lesson 4, Support: Reading scales

Unit 7

Week 1: **Number – Addition and subtraction**
Lesson 1, Support: Storeys of 10
Lesson 2, Extension: Pencil pot problems
Lesson 3, Extension: Calculation rescue
Lesson 4, Support: Bead addition and subtraction

Week 2: **Number – Addition and subtraction**
Lesson 1, Support: Apple basket addition
Lesson 2, Extension: Sea subtractions
Lesson 3, Support: Picnic problems
Lesson 4, Extension: Flag facts

Week 3: **Measurement (time)**
Lesson 1, Extension: Days and months
Lesson 2, Support: Sequencing seasons
Lesson 3, Extension: Telling the time
Lesson 4, Support: More time

Unit 8

Week 1: **Number – Number and place value**
Lesson 1, Support: Number names to 10
Lesson 2, Extension: Bowling scores
Lesson 3, Support: Supermarket counting
Lesson 4, Extension: Multiples mix-up

Week 2: **Number – Fractions**
Lesson 1, Support: Quick quarters
Lesson 2, Extension: Quarter questions
Lesson 3, Support: Cube tower quarters
Lesson 4, Extension: Picnic quarters

Week 3: **Measurement (volume and capacity)**
Lesson 1, Support: Full or empty?
Lesson 2, Extension: Comparing capacities
Lesson 3, Support: More than
Lesson 4, Extension: More, less or the same?

Unit 9

Week 1: **Number – Number and place value**
        Lesson 1, Support: Number names to 20
        Lesson 2, Extension: 10s and 1s tent
        Lesson 3, Extension: Cuckoo counting
        Lesson 4, Support: Dinosaur tracks of 2

Week 2: **Number – Addition and subtraction**
        Lesson 1, Support: Double decker doubles
        Lesson 2, Extension: Building block addition
        Lesson 3, Extension: Tricky trios
        Lesson 4, Support: Yellow submarines

Week 3: **Geometry – Position and direction**
        Lesson 1, Support: Position words
        Lesson 2, Support: Farm positions
        Lesson 3, Extension: Directions
        Lesson 4, Extension: Turning

Unit 10

Week 1: **Number – Multiplication and division, including Number and place value**
        Lesson 1, Extension: Ewe 2s
        Lesson 2, Support: Pear pairs
        Lesson 3, Extension: Hives and 10s
        Lesson 4, Support: How many?

Week 2: **Number – Multiplication and division**
        Lesson 1, Support: How many sweets?
        Lesson 2, Extension: Penny purses
        Lesson 3, Extension: Milkshake shares
        Lesson 4, Extension: Bird sharing

Week 3: **Measurement (length and height)**
        Lesson 1, Support: More or less than 1 metre?
        Lesson 2, Extension: Estimating and measuring
        Lesson 3, Extension: How many bricks?
        Lesson 4, Support: Shapes that balance

Unit 11

Week 1: **Number – Addition and subtraction**
Lesson 1, Support: Monkey-puzzle trees
Lesson 2, Extension: Magic carpet calculations
Lesson 3, Support: Seaside problems (1)
Lesson 4, Extension: Seaside problems (2)

Week 2: **Number – Addition and subtraction**
Lesson 1, Support: Penny problems
Lesson 2, Extension: Pizza toppings
Lesson 3, Support: Tremendous trios
Lesson 4, Extension: 10 more or less town

Week 3: **Geometry – Position of shape**
Lesson 1, Extension: 2-D shape patterns
Lesson 2, Extension: Drawing 2-D shapes
Lesson 3, Support: 3-D shape patterns and models
Lesson 4, Support: 3-D shape match

Unit 12

Week 1: **Number – Multiplication and division**
Lesson 1, Support: Treasure doubles
Lesson 2, Extension: Spotted hanky halves
Lesson 3, Support: Fraction flags
Lesson 4, Extension: Half and quarter constellations

Week 2: **Number – Fractions**
Lesson 1, Support: Finding fractions
Lesson 2, Extension: Button halves and quarters
Lesson 3, Support: Four flag fractions
Lesson 4, Extension: Collect the marbles!

Week 3: **Measurement (time)**
Lesson 1, Support: My day
Lesson 2, Extension: Drawing hands
Lesson 3, Support: Things I can do in 1 minute
Lesson 4, Extension: Train times

Name: _____ Date: _____

Missing numbers

Read and write numbers 0 to 20

0 1 ☐ ☐ 4

1 ☐ 3 ☐ 5 ☐

3 ☐ ☐ 6 7

5 6 ☐ ☐ 9 ☐

☐ 7 8 ☐ ☐

Teacher's notes

Children complete the sequence of numbers in each row by writing in the missing numbers. All the sequences are within the range 0–10.

Name: _____ Date: _____

1 more, 1 less

Find 1 more or 1 less than a number

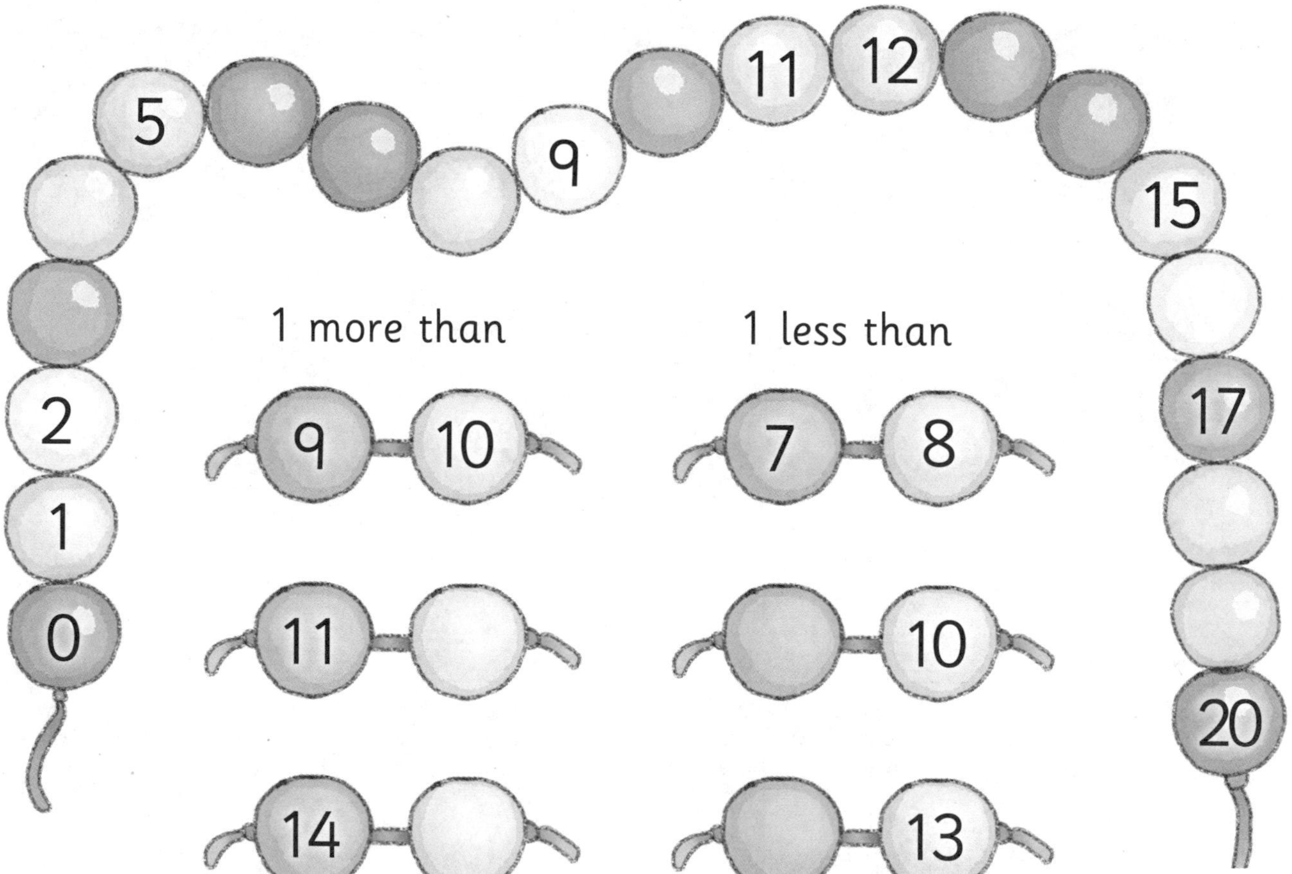

5   9   11   12   15

2   1   0   17   20

1 more than	1 less than
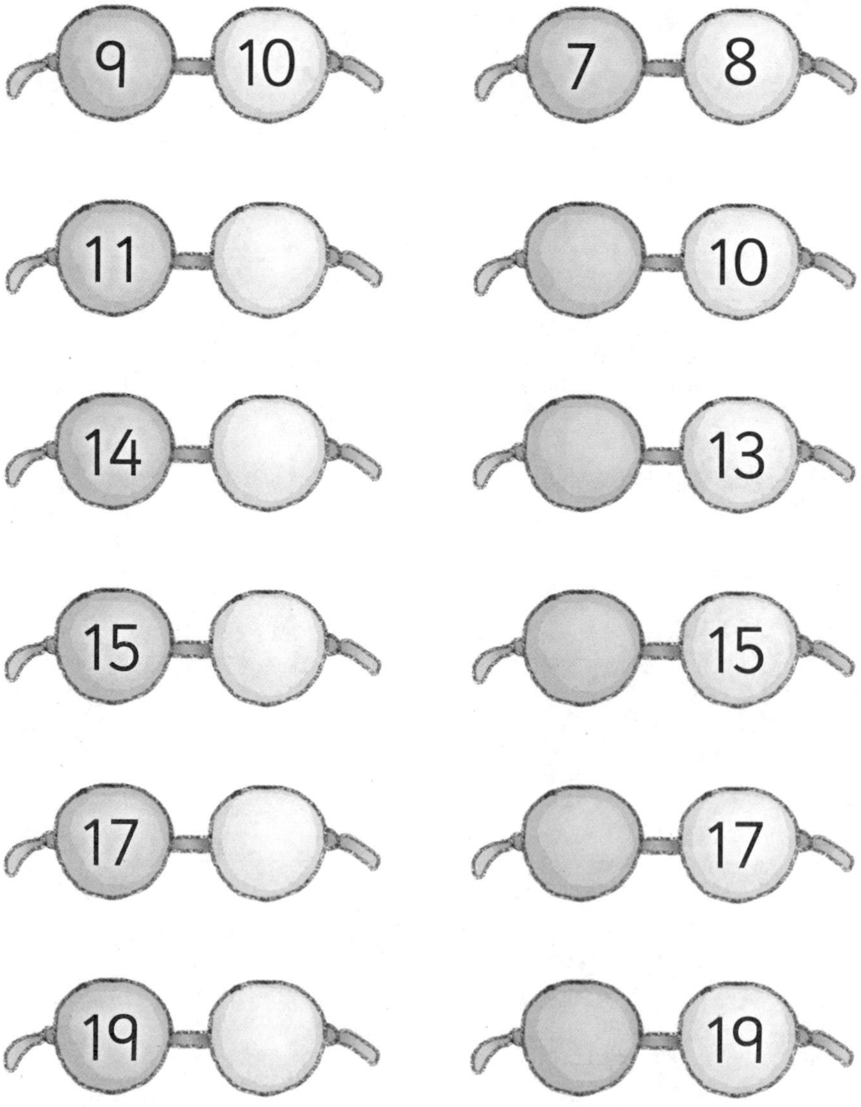 9 10	7 8
11 ⬜	⬜ 10
14 ⬜	⬜ 13
15 ⬜	⬜ 15
17 ⬜	⬜ 17
19 ⬜	⬜ 19

Teacher's notes

Children write the missing numbers on the long string of beads to complete the sequence 0–20. Then, for the pairs of beads with a number shown on the first column of beads, they write the number which is one more. For the pairs with a number shown on the second column of beads, they write the number which is one less. Remind the children that they can use their 0–20 string to help them, if needed.

Name: _____ Date: _____

Counting cupcakes

Count numbers from 0 to 20

You will need:
- scissors
- glue

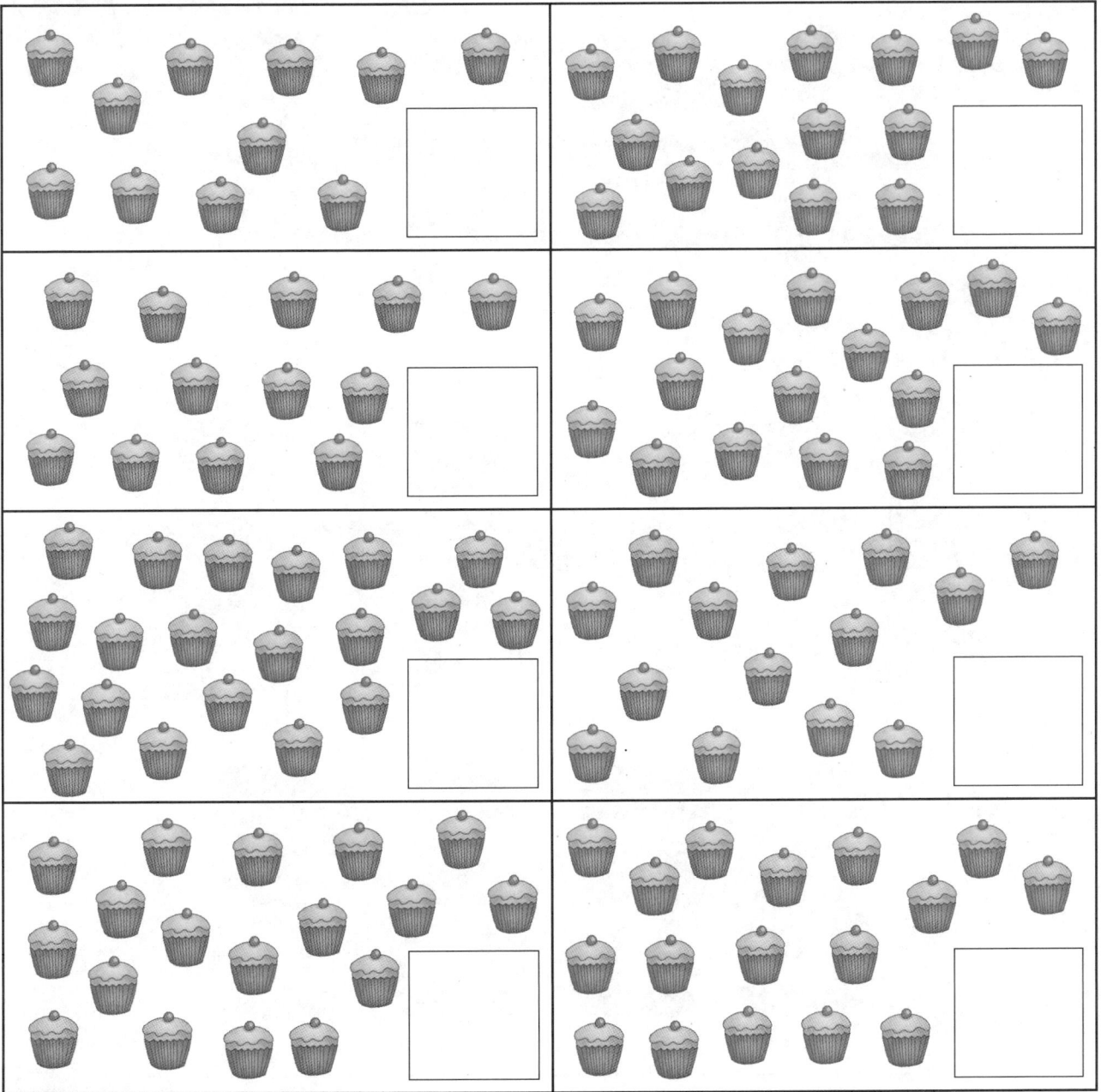

Children cut out the numbers at the bottom of the sheet. They count the number of cupcakes in each set and stick the correct number next to it. Once they have completed this activity, ask children to identify the two numbers from 11–20 that are missing and draw the two sets on the back of this sheet.

| 11 | 13 | 14 | 15 | 16 | 17 | 18 | 20 |

Name: _____ Date: _____

Number race

Order numbers up to 20

START   9   10   FINISH

START   12   13   FINISH

START   16   17   FINISH

1st   2nd   3rd

Teacher's notes

Children complete the three number sequences. They then look at the ordinal number for each race, and write in the number of the competitor who finished in that position.

Name: _____ Date: _____

How many hens?

Make addition number sentences to 5 by joining groups

☐ + ☐ = ☐

☐ + ☐ = ☐

☐ + ☐ = ☐

☐ + ☐ = ☐

Teacher's notes

Children complete the addition calculations by counting the shaded hens and white hens and writing the numbers in the boxes provided. They then write the total in the last box.

Name: _____ Date: _____

Kangaroo addition

Make addition number sentences to 6 by counting on

2 jumps forward

$\boxed{}$ $\bigoplus$ $\boxed{}$ $\bigodot$ $\boxed{}$

3 jumps forward

$\boxed{}$ $\bigcirc$ $\boxed{}$ $\bigcirc$ $\boxed{}$

1 jump forward

$\boxed{}$ $\bigcirc$ $\boxed{}$ $\bigcirc$ $\boxed{}$

2 jumps forward

$\boxed{}$ $\bigcirc$ $\boxed{}$ $\bigcirc$ $\boxed{}$

2 jumps forward

$\boxed{}$ $\bigcirc$ $\boxed{}$ $\bigcirc$ $\boxed{}$

Teacher's notes

For each picture, children use the number of the box the kangaroo is standing on, the number of jumps it takes and the number of the box it lands on to complete the addition calculation.

Name: _____ Date: _____

Cakes away!

Make subtraction number sentences to 5 by taking away

You will need:
- scissors
- glue

$3 - 2 =$ ☐

$3 - 3 =$ ☐

$4 - 2 =$ ☐

$4 - 1 =$ ☐

   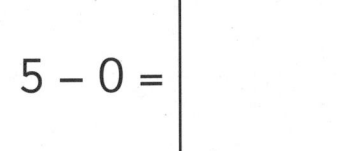

$5 - 0 =$ ☐

$5 - 1 =$ ☐

Teacher's notes

Children cut out the cakes at the bottom of the sheet. They work out the answer to each subtraction calculation, crossing out the number of cakes to be 'taken away' as shown in the example. They then glue the cake showing the correct answer in the correct space.

2   5   1   4   0   3

Name: _____ Date: _____

Jumping back

Make subtraction number sentences to 5 by counting back

3 jumps back

$$5 \; - \; 3 \; = \; \boxed{}$$

4 jumps back

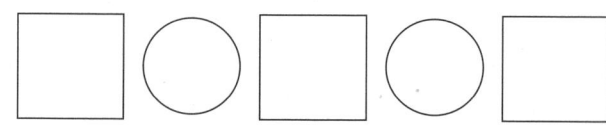

3 jumps back

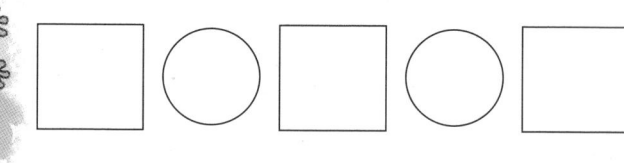

4 jumps back

2 jumps back

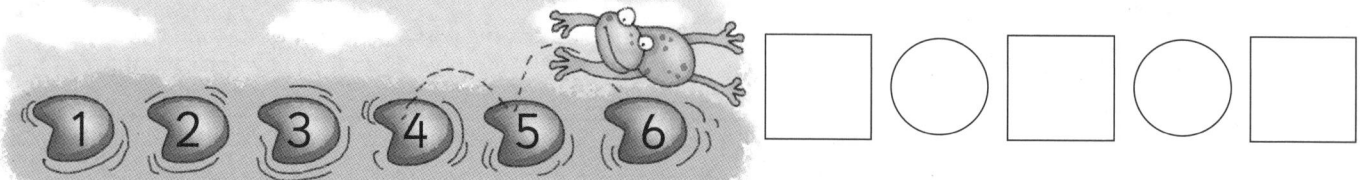

Teacher's notes

For each picture, children use the number of the lily pad the frog is sitting on, the number of jumps back it takes and the number of the lily pad it lands on to complete the subtraction calculation.

Name: _____ Date: _____

Shape names

Know circles, triangles, squares, rectangles, stars and hexagons

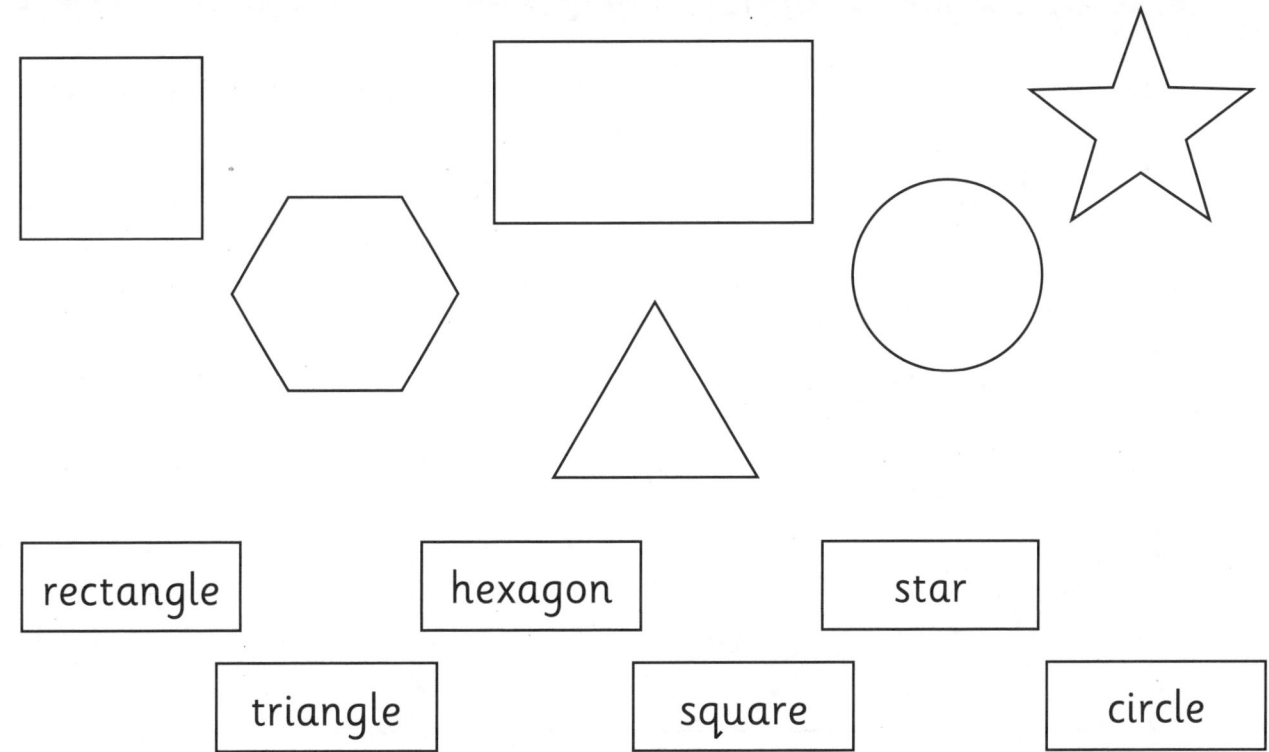

rectangle		hexagon		star	
	triangle		square		circle

	Number of sides	**Number of corners**
circle		
triangle		
rectangle		
square		
hexagon		
star		

Teacher's notes

Children draw a line to match each shape and name. They then count and write how many sides and corners each shape has in the table.

Name: _____ Date: _____

Face shapes

Spot circles, triangles, squares, rectangles, stars and hexagons

You will need:
• coloured pencils

circle   hexagon   triangle   star   rectangle   square

Teacher's notes
Children use a different colour to draw a ring around each shape at the top of the sheet. They then colour the shapes in the picture to match.

Name: _____ Date: _____

Triangles

Know how to draw triangles

You will need:
- coloured pencils
- ruler

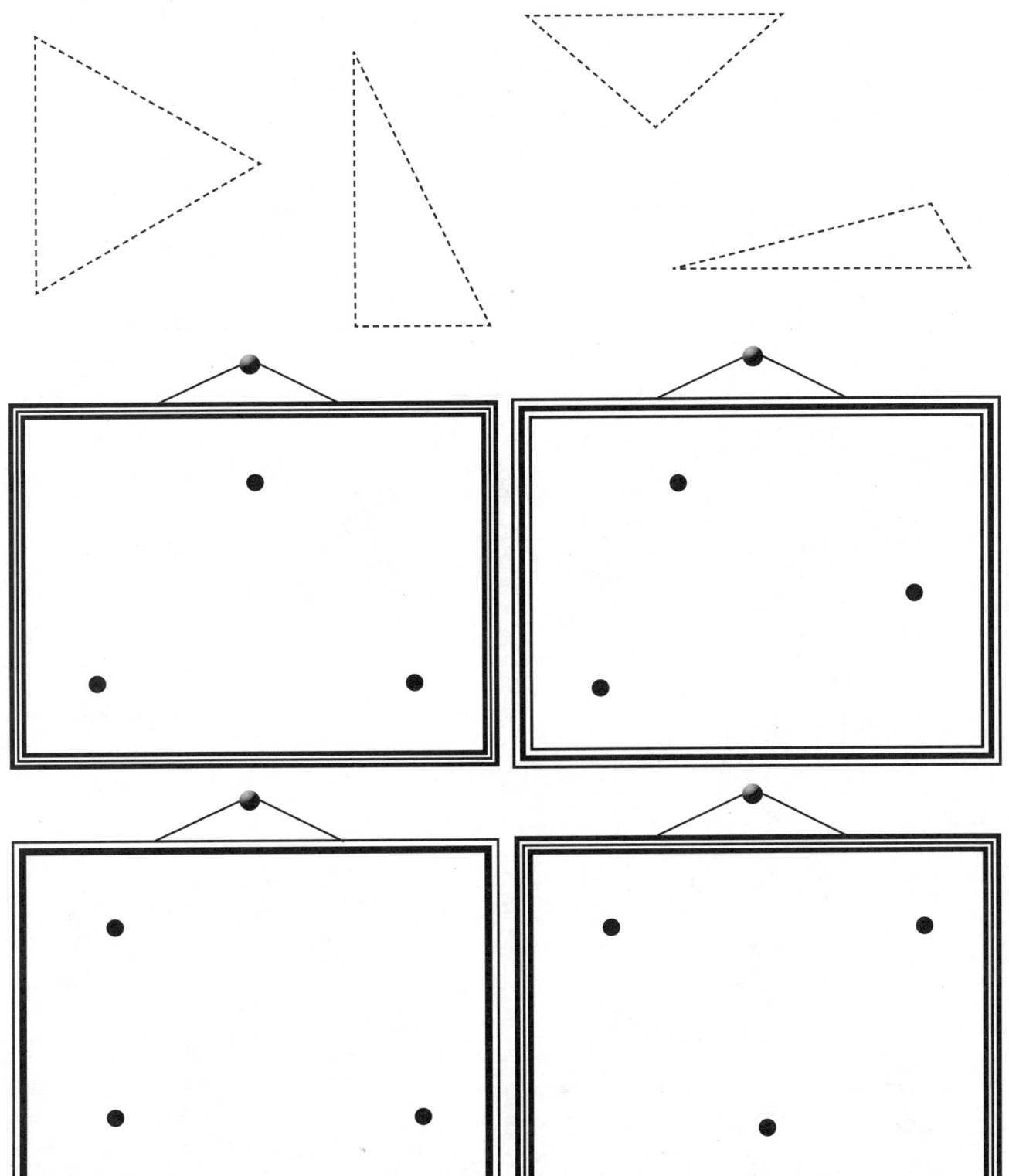

Teacher's notes

Children trace over the dashed lines to draw the first group of triangles. They then draw the second group of triangles by joining each set of three dots with straight lines.

Name: _____ Date: _____

Rectangle or square?

Know and draw rectangles and squares

You will need:
• two coloured pencils

This is a

r_____ .

This is a

s_____ .

Teacher's notes

Children trace over the dashed lines to draw the square and rectangle, shade each one a different colour and then complete the sentences to name them. They then colour the shapes in the picture to match their coloured square and rectangle.

Name: _____ **Date:** _____

Adding to 5

Know addition facts to 5

0	1	2	3	4	5

3 + 1 = ☐   1 + 4 = ☐

0 + 2 = ☐   0 + 3 = ☐

2 + 1 = ☐   2 + 0 = ☐

0 + 5 = ☐   2 + 3 = ☐

1 + 0 = ☐   0 + 3 = ☐

4 + 0 = ☐   3 + 2 = ☐

1 + 2 = ☐   5 + 0 = ☐

0 + 4 = ☐   0 + 1 = ☐

2 + 2 = ☐   1 + 3 = ☐

4 + 1 = ☐   2 + 3 = ☐

Teacher's notes

Children complete the addition calculations. They can use the number track and pictures to help support their working.

Name: _____ Date: _____

Dice subtraction

Know subtraction facts to 10

You will need:
- 1–6 dice
- ruler

6 − ☐ = ☐   6 − ☐ = ☐

7 − ☐ = ☐   7 − ☐ = ☐

8 − ☐ = ☐   8 − ☐ = ☐

9 − ☐ = ☐   9 − ☐ = ☐

10 − ☐ = ☐   10 − ☐ = ☐

Teacher's notes

Children roll a 1–6 dice. They write the number rolled on a blank dice, then write the answer to the subtraction calculation. They repeat until each calculation shows a different subtraction fact.

Name: _____ Date: _____

Twins totals

Know addition doubles to 5 + 5

☐ + ☐ = ☐

☐ + ☐ = ☐

☐ + ☐ = ☐

☐ + ☐ = ☐

☐ + ☐ = ☐

Teacher's notes

For each set of twins, children colour and count the candles on the birthday cakes. They then find the total number of candles and write the addition double.

Name: _____ Date: _____

Baking away

Use subtraction facts to 10 to find addition facts

4 – ☐ = 3

☐ + ☐ = ☐

5 – ☐ = 2

☐ + ☐ = ☐

---

2 – ☐ = 2

☐ + ☐ = ☐

6 – ☐ = 3

☐ + ☐ = ☐

---

7 – ☐ = 0

☐ + ☐ = ☐

Teacher's notes

Children complete each subtraction calculation and then write the related addition calculation.

Name: _____ Date: _____

Skateboard number tracks

Add two numbers that total up to 10

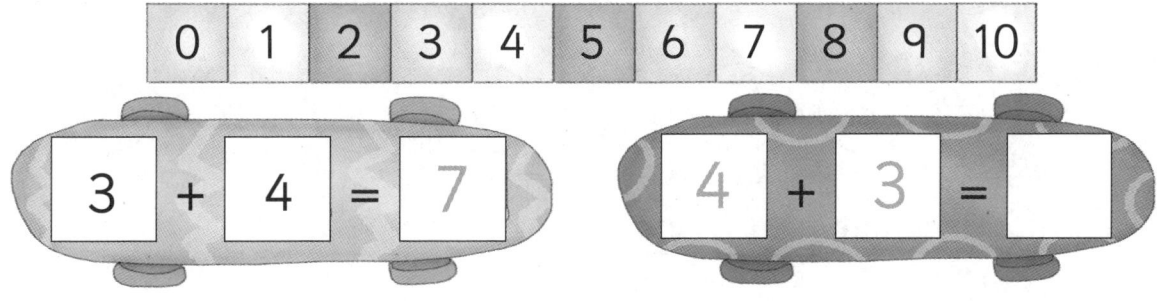

| 0 | 1 | 2 | 3 | 4 | 5 | 6 | 7 | 8 | 9 | 10 |

3 + 4 = 7   4 + 3 =

| 0 | 1 | 2 | 3 | 4 | 5 | 6 | 7 | 8 | 9 | 10 |

2 + 4 =   ☐ + ☐ =

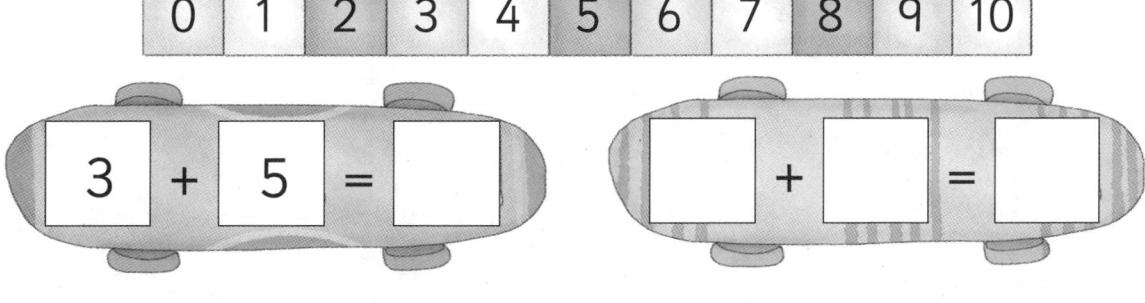

| 0 | 1 | 2 | 3 | 4 | 5 | 6 | 7 | 8 | 9 | 10 |

3 + 5 =   ☐ + ☐ =

| 0 | 1 | 2 | 3 | 4 | 5 | 6 | 7 | 8 | 9 | 10 |

2 + 7 =   ☐ + ☐ =

Teacher's notes

Children complete the first addition calculation, if necessary drawing 'jumps' on the number track to show how to count on to find the answer. They then change the order in which the numbers are added, complete the second calculation and, if necessary, check their answer on the number track.

Name: _____ Date: _____

Bees and flowers

Find the difference between two numbers

① ② ③ ④ ⑤ ⑥ ⑦ ⑧ ⑨ ⑩

The difference between 6 and 2 is ☐ .

① ② ③ ④ ⑤ ⑥ ⑦ ⑧ ⑨ ⑩

The difference between 8 and 3 is ☐ .

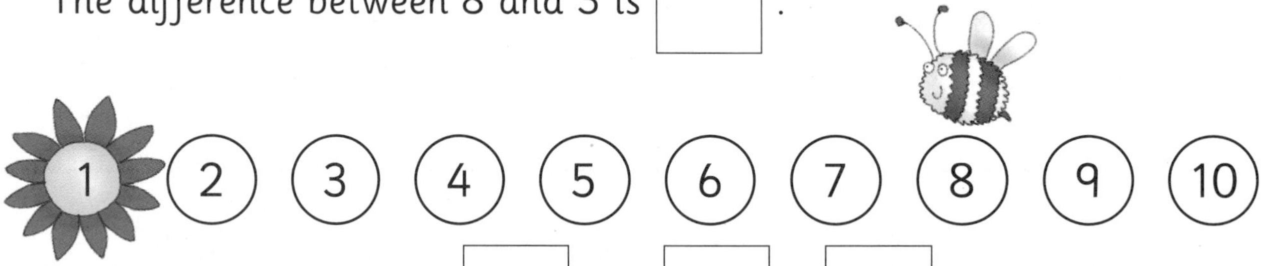

① ② ③ ④ ⑤ ⑥ ⑦ ⑧ ⑨ ⑩

The difference between ☐ and ☐ is ☐ .

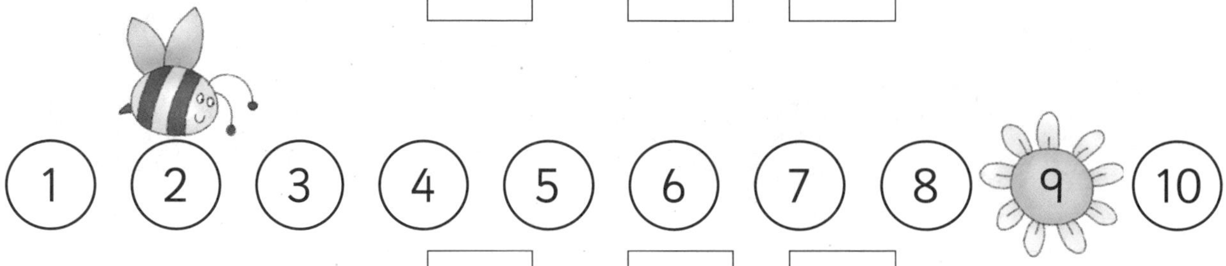

① ② ③ ④ ⑤ ⑥ ⑦ ⑧ ⑨ ⑩

The difference between ☐ and ☐ is ☐ .

① ② ③ ④ ⑤ ⑥ ⑦ ⑧ ⑨ ⑩

The difference between ☐ and ☐ is ☐ .

Teacher's notes

On each number track, children draw the jumps the bee must make to reach the flower. They count the number of jumps and complete the sentence to show the difference between the two numbers.

Name: _____ Date: _____

Sandcastle subtraction and addition

Solve missing number problems

$3 + 2 = \boxed{}$

$6 - 5 = \boxed{}$

$6 + \boxed{} = 9$

$7 - \boxed{} = 5$

$4 + \boxed{} = 8$

$8 - \boxed{} = 8$

$3 + \boxed{} = 10$

$9 - \boxed{} = 3$

$5 + \boxed{} = 10$

$10 - \boxed{} = 4$

Teacher's notes

For each addition or subtraction calculation, children write the missing number in the space provided.

Name: _____ Date: _____

How many?

Solve addition and subtraction problems

Asha has 3 cars.

Ellis has 4 cars.

How many cars altogether?

 + 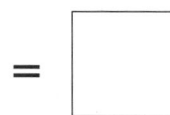 =

Mani has 8 cakes.

He gives 5 to his friends.
How many cakes are left?

 −  =

There are 9 cats on the wall.

4 jumped off.
How many cats are left?

☐ − ☐ = ☐

Laura has 5 pencils.

She finds 5 more.

How many pencils altogether?

☐ + ☐ = ☐

Teacher's notes

Children complete the calculation for each problem in the spaces provided.

Name: _____   Date: _____

Which is longest?

Talk about and compare lengths

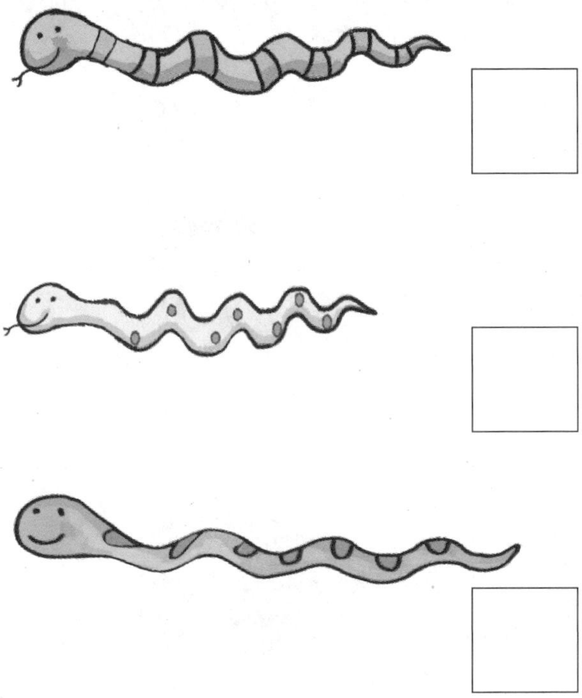

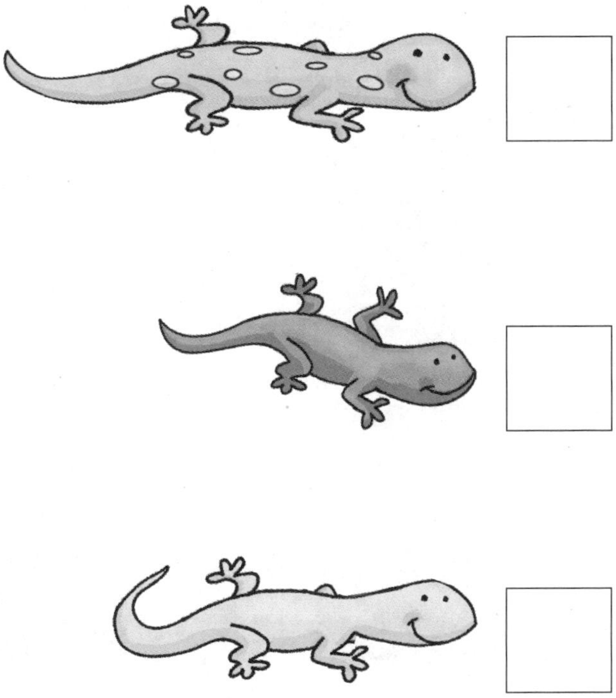

Children number the animals in each row from shortest to longest, numbering the shortest 1 and the longest 3.

Name: _____ Date: _____

Which is the tallest?

Talk about and compare heights

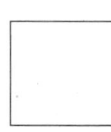

Teacher's notes

In each row of animals, children label the tallest animal 'T' and the shortest 'S'.

Name: _____ **Date:** _____

Measuring with hands

Measure lengths, widths and heights

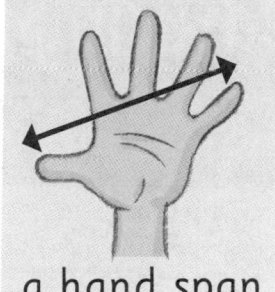

a hand span

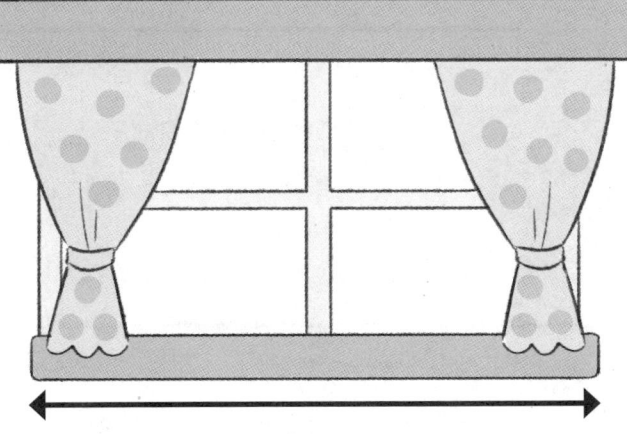

I measured [ ] spans.

I measured [ ] spans.

I measured [ ] spans.

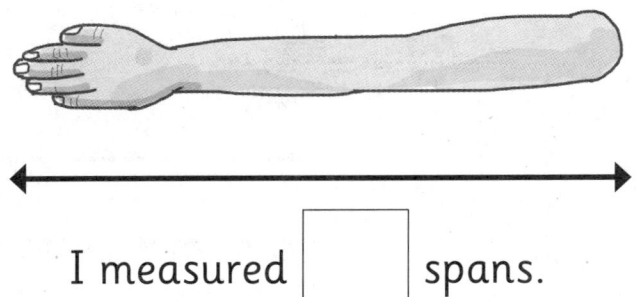

I measured [ ] spans.

I measured [ ] spans.

Teacher's notes

Ensure children have access to each of the objects shown. They measure and record each length, width or height, in hand spans.

Name: _____ Date: _____

Measuring length, width and height

You will need:
• ruler

Use a ruler to measure length, width and height

_____

☐ centimetres

_____

☐ centimetres

_____

☐ centimetres

_____

☐ centimetres

☐ centimetres long

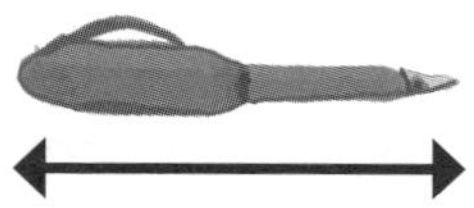

☐ centimetres long

☐ centimetres tall

☐ centimetres wide

| Teacher's notes |
Children use a ruler to measure each line and record the length. Next, they measure the length, width or height of the objects shown and record each measurement next to the appropriate picture.

Name: _____ **Date:** _____

Scarf patterns

Count in 2s

0 | 2 | 4 | | | 10

10 | 8 | | | | 0

10 | | 14 | | |

20 | | | | 8

0 | | | | | | | | 20

Name: _____ Date: _____

Flower garden 5s

Count in 5s

0 1 2 3 4 ☐ 6 7 8 9 ☐ 11 12 13 14 ☐ 16 17 18 19 ☐

0   5   ☐   ☐   ☐

0   ☐   ☐   ☐   20

0 1 2 3 4 5 6 7 8 9 10 11 12 13 14 15 16 17 18 19 20

Teacher's notes

On each number line, children draw jumps of 5 made by the insect, starting from 0. On the first three number lines, they write the missing numbers. On the last, they colour the flowers and numbers the insect lands on.

Name: _____ Date: _____

Table tennis 10s

Count on in 10s

You will need:
- scissors
- glue

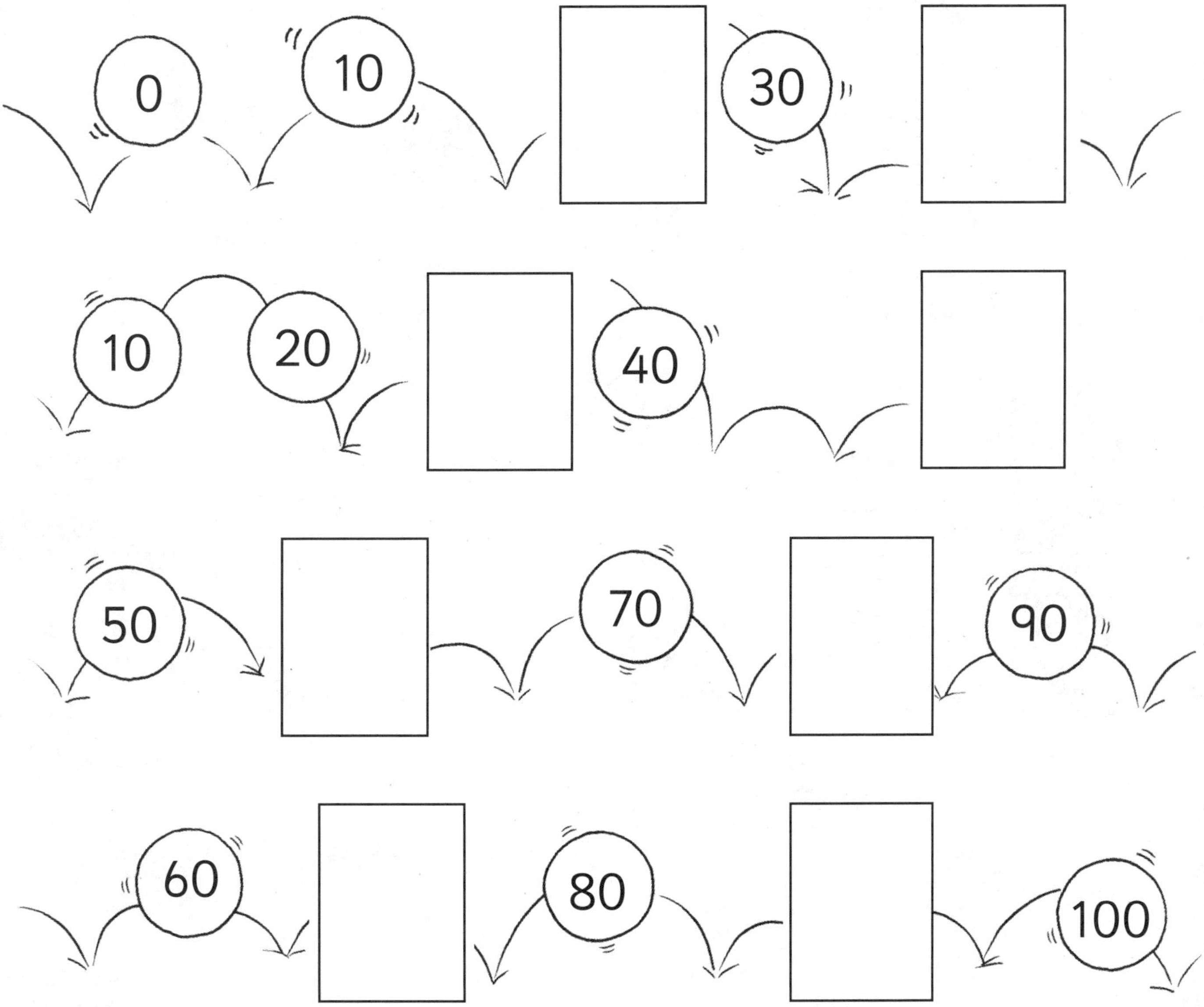

0   10   [ ]   30   [ ]

10   20   [ ]   40   [ ]

50   [ ]   70   [ ]   90

60   [ ]   80   [ ]   100

Teacher's notes

Children cut out the multiples of 10 table tennis bats at the bottom of the sheet. They stick each one into the correct position in the sequences.

20   30   50   60   90   40   70   80

Name: _____ Date: _____

Pathway patterns

Count in 2s, 5s or 10s

You will need:
• coloured pencil

fives!

twos!

tens!

Name: _____ Date: _____

How many socks?

Count sets of 2

You will need:
• coloured pencils

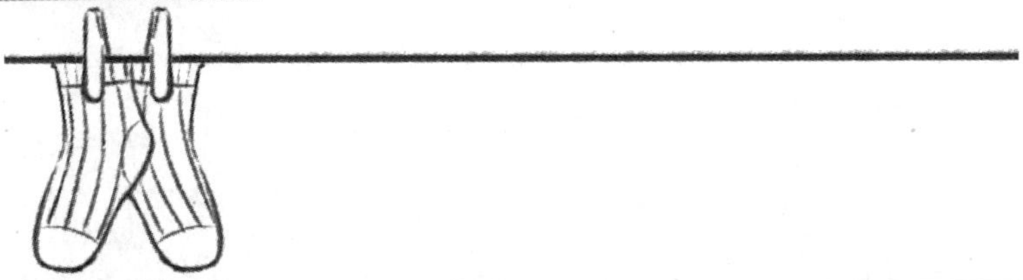

2	4	6	8	10

1	pair has

2	socks.

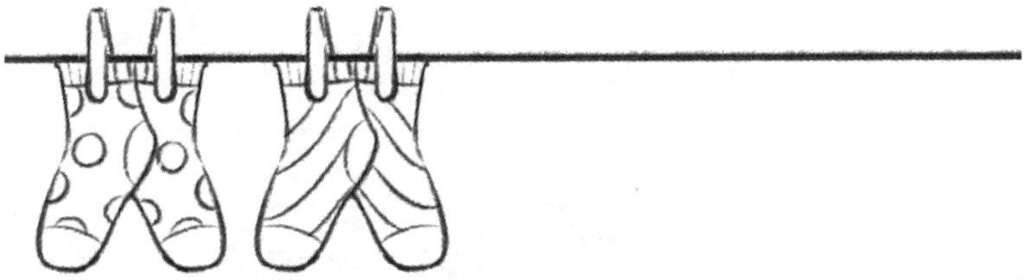

2	4	6	8	10

	pairs have

	socks.

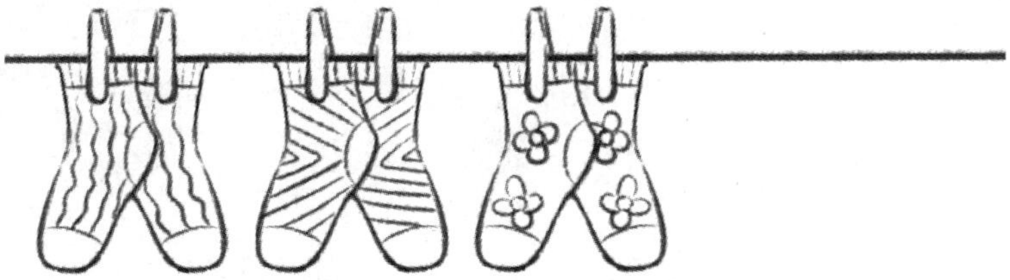

2	4		8	10

	pairs have

	socks.

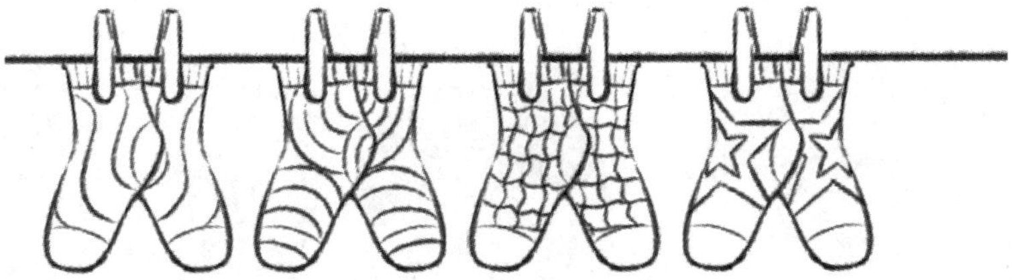

2	4	6		10

	pairs have

	socks.

2	4	6	8	

	pairs have

	socks.

Teacher's notes

Children work out how many socks there are on each washing line. They colour the steps and complete each number track. They then complete each sentence with the correct numbers.

Name: _____   Date: _____

Sticker sets

Count sets of 5

Leon has ☐ stickers.

Mia has ☐ stickers.

Caie has ☐ stickers.

Ayesha has ☐ stickers.

Emma has ☐ stickers.

Cavan has ☐ stickers.

Name: _____ Date: _____

Toffee 10s

Count sets of 10

You will need:
• coloured pencils

10	20	30	40	50

| 1 | bag of sweets makes |

| 10 | sweets altogether. |

 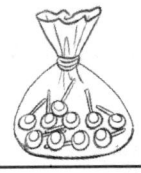

10	20	30	40	50

| | bags of sweets makes |

| | sweets altogether. |

  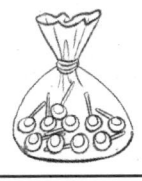

10	20		40	50

| | bags of sweets makes |

| | sweets altogether. |

 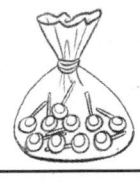  

10	20	30		50

| | bags of sweets makes |

| | sweets altogether. |

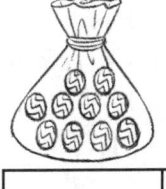 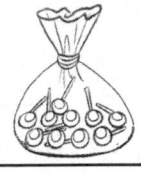   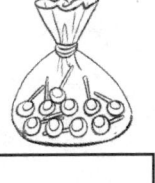

10	20	30	40	

| | bags of sweets makes |

| | sweets altogether. |

Teacher's notes

There are 10 sweets in each bag. Children work out how many sweets are in each group. They colour the steps and complete each number track, then complete each sentence with the correct numbers.

Name: _____ Date: _____

Sheep sharing

Share into equal sets

You will need:
• four different
  coloured pencils

2 groups!

[ ] sheep
in each group.

3 groups!

[ ] sheep
in each group.

3 groups!

[ ] sheep
in each group.

4 groups!

[ ] sheep
in each group.

Teacher's notes

Children share the sheep in each field into the correct number of groups by making each set a different colour. They write the number of sheep in each group in the space provided.

Name: _____ Date: _____

Beach directions

Understand 'left', 'right', 'up' and 'down'

left ←

right →

up ↑

down ↓

Teacher's notes

At the bottom of the page, children draw a line to match each object to the direction the boy has to look to find it in the scene at the top.

Name: _____ Date: _____

Where is it?

Understand and use position words

| middle | bottom | top |

What is below the  ?

What is above the  ?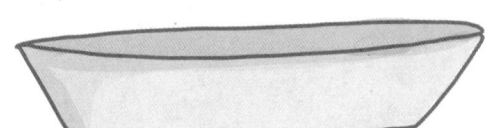

What is between the  and the  ?

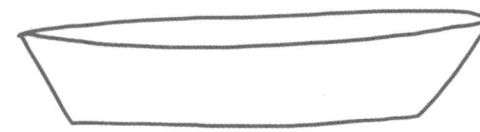

Name: _____ Date: _____

Whole and half turns

Know whole and half turns

You will need:
- coloured pencils

half turn

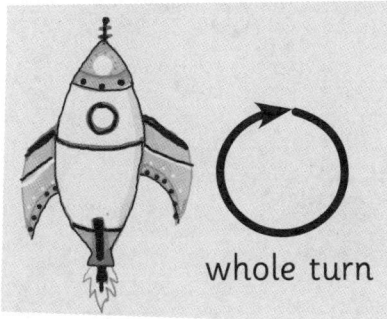

whole turn

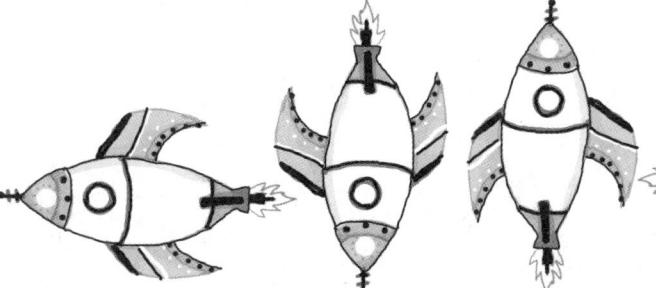

whole turn

half turn

whole turn

half turn

Teacher's notes

Children draw a ring around the pictures that show the correct amount of turn for the teddy and rocket.
They then draw the tree and ice-cream after they have made a whole turn and a half turn.

Name: _____ Date: _____

Quarter and three-quarter turns

Know quarter and three-quarter turns

quarter turn

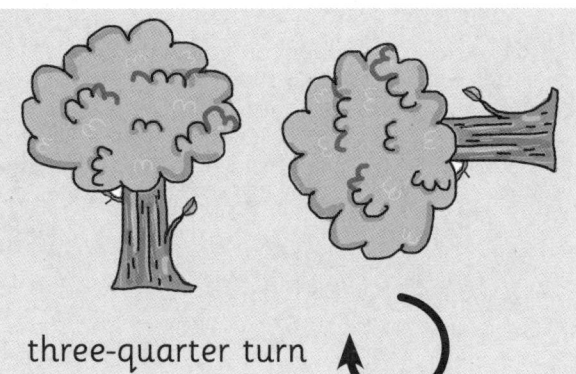

three-quarter turn

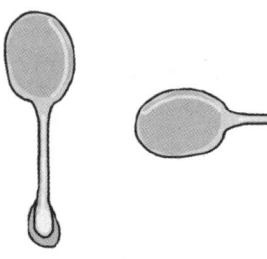 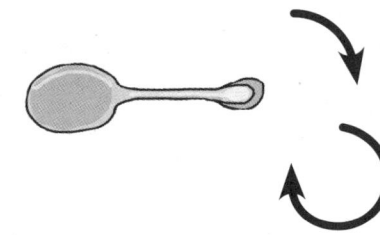

Teacher's notes

Children draw a ring around the arrow that shows the size of turn the object has made (quarter or three quarter).

Name: _____ Date: _____

How many monkeys?

Know addition facts to 15

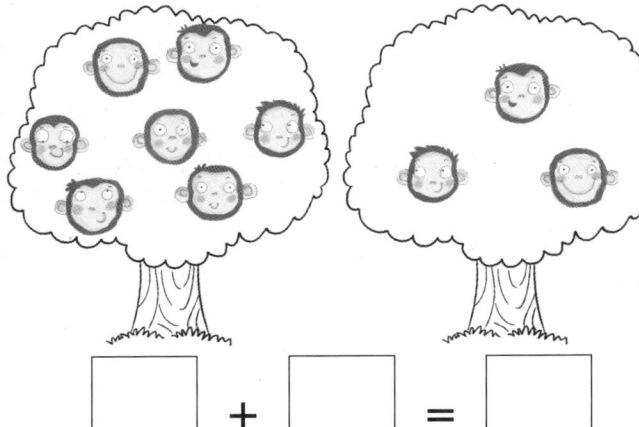

☐ + ☐ = ☐

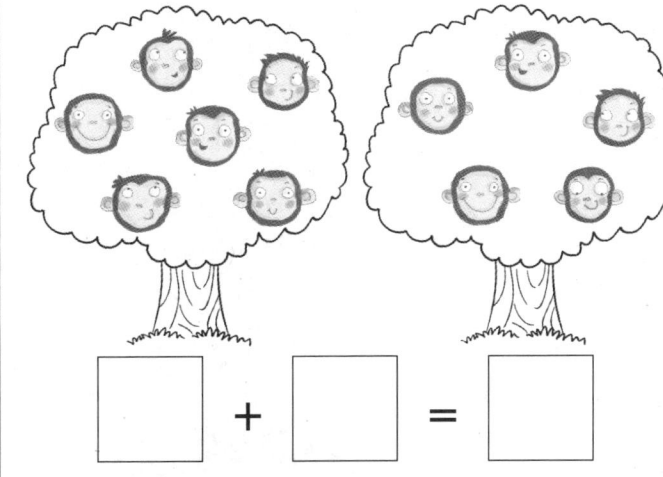

☐ + ☐ = ☐

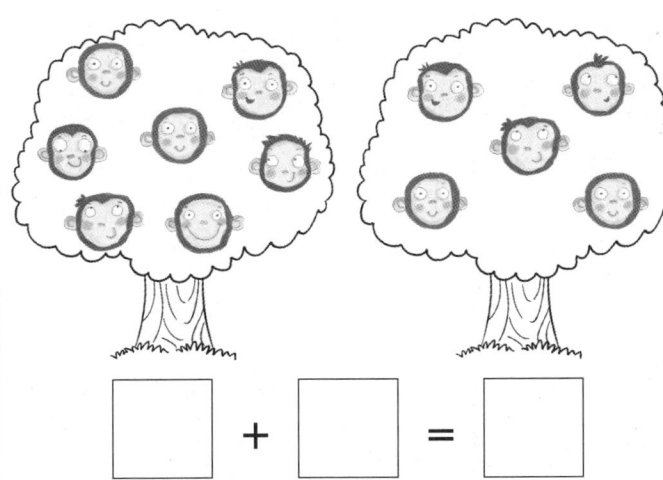

☐ + ☐ = ☐

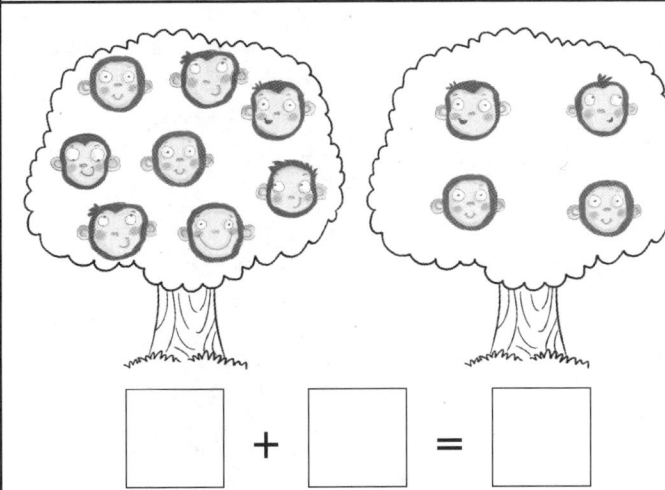

☐ + ☐ = ☐

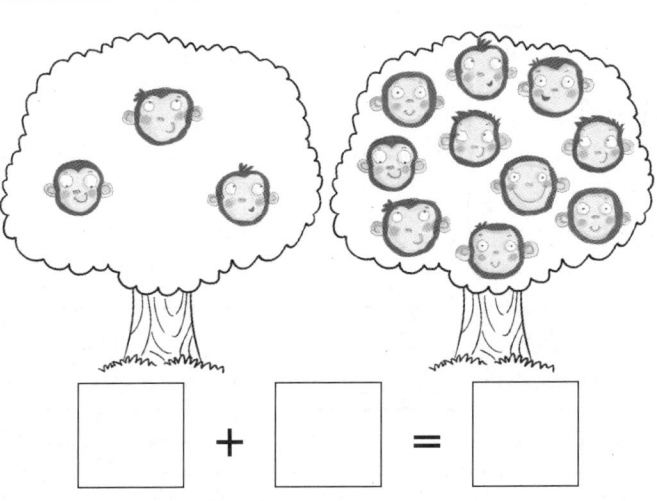

☐ + ☐ = ☐

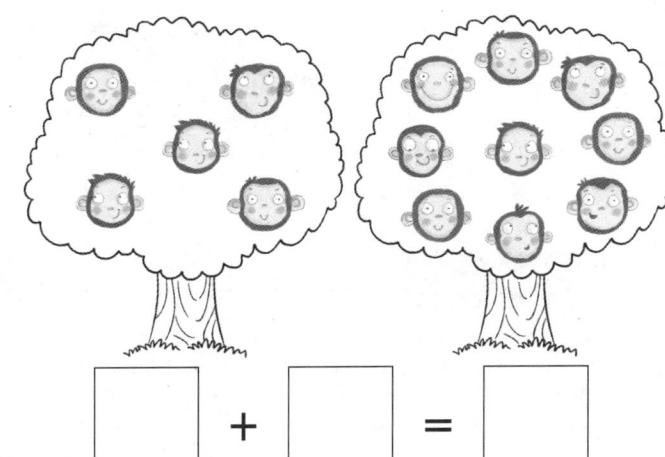

☐ + ☐ = ☐

Teacher's notes

Children count the number of monkeys in each tree and write it in one of the spaces provided. They find the total number of monkeys and complete the addition calculation.

Name: _____ Date: _____

Spider subtraction

Know subtraction facts to 15

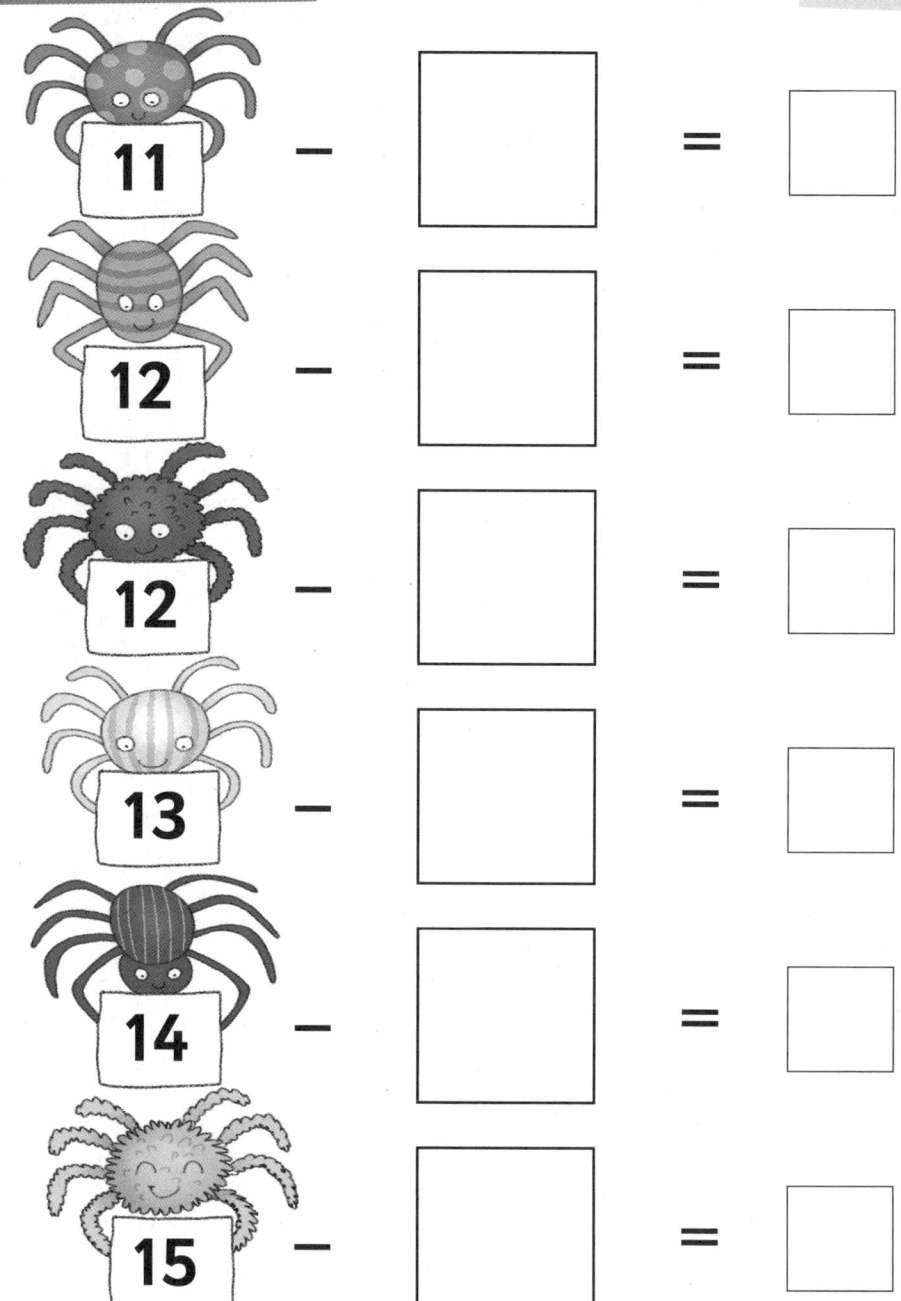

11 − ☐ = ☐

12 − ☐ = ☐

12 − ☐ = ☐

13 − ☐ = ☐

14 − ☐ = ☐

15 − ☐ = ☐

Teacher's notes

Children cut the cobwebs from the bottom of the sheet and use them to make their own subtraction calculations, gluing each one next to a spider. They solve each calculation and write the answer.

6   8   7   10   9   11

Name: _____ Date: _____

Missing number muddle

Find the missing number

You will need:
- scissors
- glue

| 1 | 2 | 3 | 4 | 5 | 6 | 7 | 8 | 9 | 10 | 11 | 12 | 13 | 14 | 15 |

6 + ☐ = 10   10 − ☐ = 8

4 + ☐ = 11   11 − ☐ = 10

7 + ☐ = 10   10 − ☐ = 2

8 + ☐ = 12   12 − ☐ = 6

9 + ☐ = 14   13 − ☐ = 8

Teacher's notes

Children cut the numbers from the bottom of the sheet and glue them into the correct place to complete each calculation, if necessary using the number track to support their thinking.

| 4 | 8 | 7 | 4 | 6 |
| 2 | 5 | 3 | 1 | 5 |

Name: _____ Date: _____

How many are there?

Solve word problems

There were
14 cherries on
the plate.

Samir ate 5.

How many were left?

☐ ◯ ☐ ◯ ☐

Hattie
threaded
8 beads onto
a lace.
Then she threaded 5 more.

How many beads altogether?

☐ ◯ ☐ ◯ ☐

Amir baked 15 cakes.

He gave 4 to his friends.

How many cakes were left?

☐ ◯ ☐ ◯ ☐

Maya put 10 books
on the shelf.

Then she put
4 more on.

How many books altogether?

☐ ◯ ☐ ◯ ☐

_____

_____

☐ ◯ ☐ ◯ ☐

Teacher's notes

Children write the addition or subtraction calculation for each problem, then write and draw their own problem in the space provided.

Name: _____ Date: _____

Fruit fractions

Find half of a shape

You will need:
- scissors
- glue

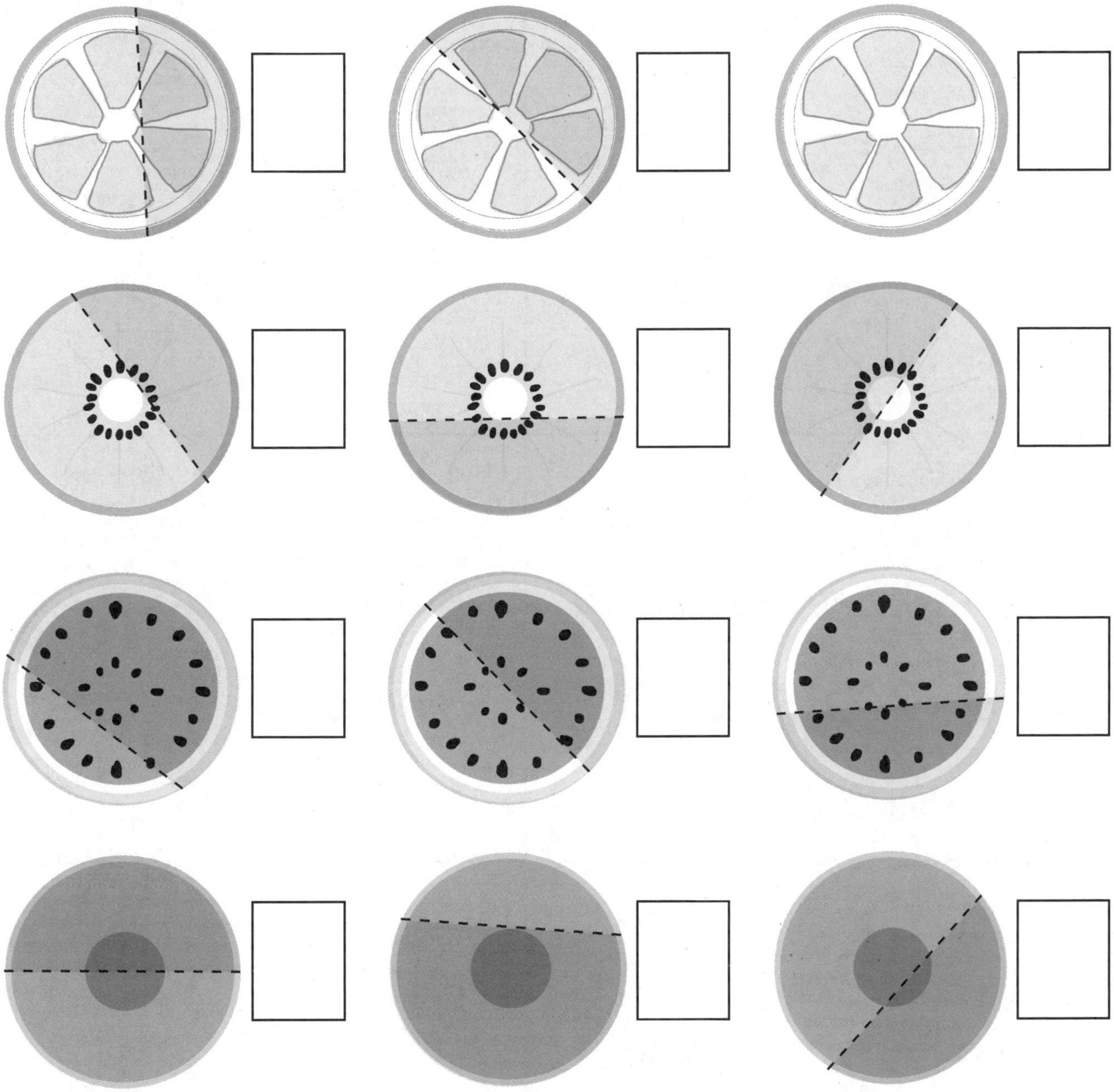

Teacher's notes

Children cut the labels from the bottom of the sheet and glue them onto the box beside the fruit in each row that has been cut exactly in half.

$\frac{1}{2}$ | $\frac{1}{2}$ | half | half

Name: _____ Date: _____

Honeybee halves

Find half of a set of objects

Half of 2 is ☐ .

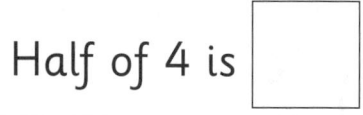

Half of 4 is ☐ .

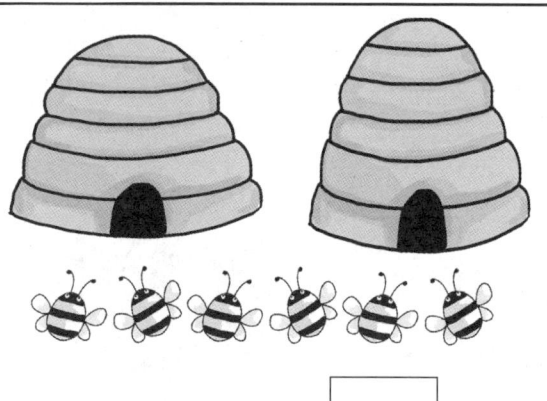

Half of 6 is ☐ .

Half of 8 is ☐ .

Half of 10 is ☐ .

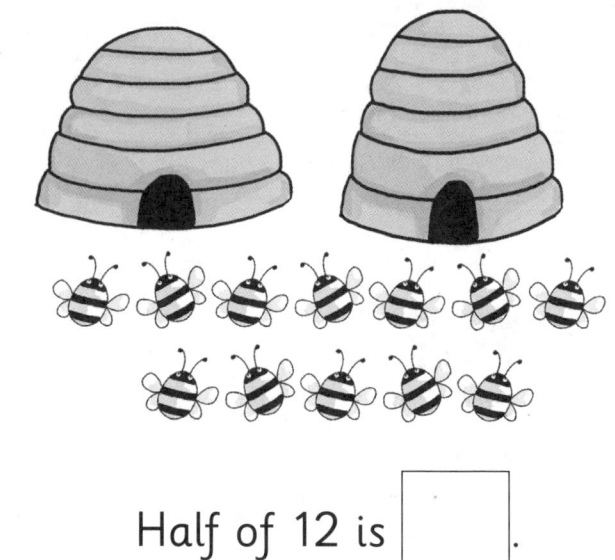

Half of 12 is ☐ .

Teacher's notes

Children draw lines to show half of the bees flying to one hive and half to the other. They work out how many bees fly to each hive and complete the sentence.

Name: _____ Date: _____

Cube tower halves

Find half of a length

You will need:
- coloured pencils

Name: _____ Date: _____

Half measures

Combine halves to make one whole

Jed has snapped his pencil in half.

Measure it and work out how long it was.

 ☐ centimetres long

---

The sandwiches have all been halved.

How many whole sandwiches are there?

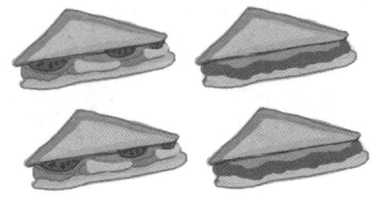 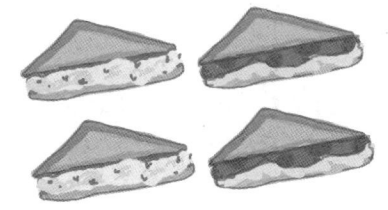 ☐ sandwiches

---

Half of the jars of jam have been sold.

How many jars of jam were there?

 ☐ jars

---

This bean plant is half as
tall as it will ever grow.

Measure the bean plant.

How tall will it grow?

☐ centimetres tall

Name: _____ **Date:** _____

Going shopping

Use coins to pay for items

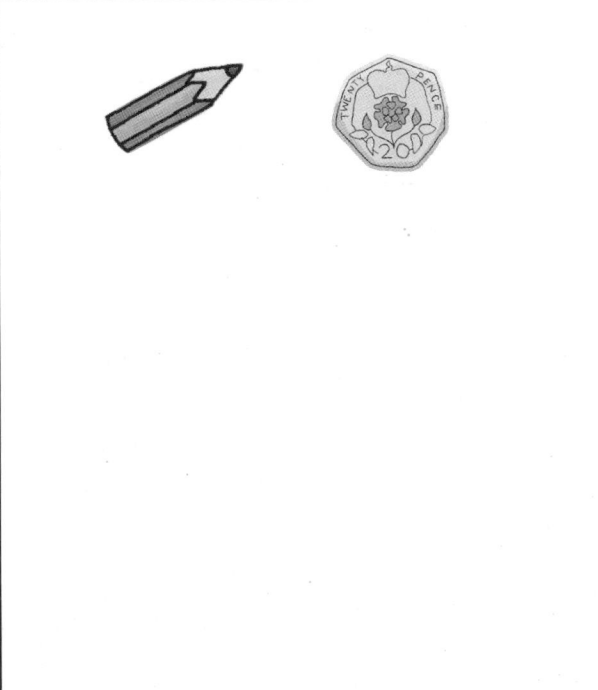

Teacher's notes

Children look at the coin needed to pay for each item. They find another way of paying for the item using different coins and draw the coins in the box. Allow the children to use coins if necessary.

Name: _____ Date: _____

Same amounts

Use coins to pay for items

You will need:
• 1p coins

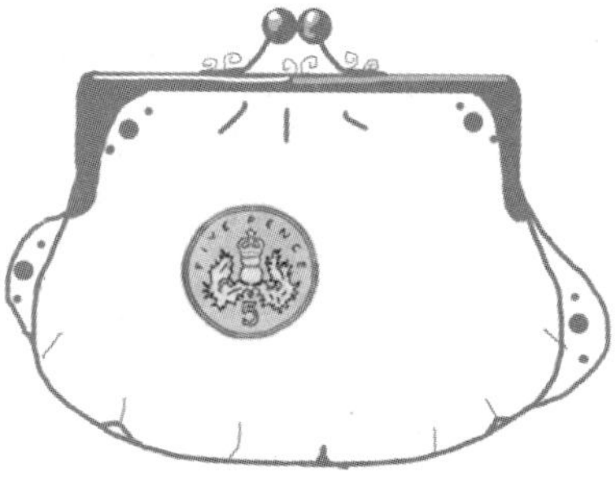

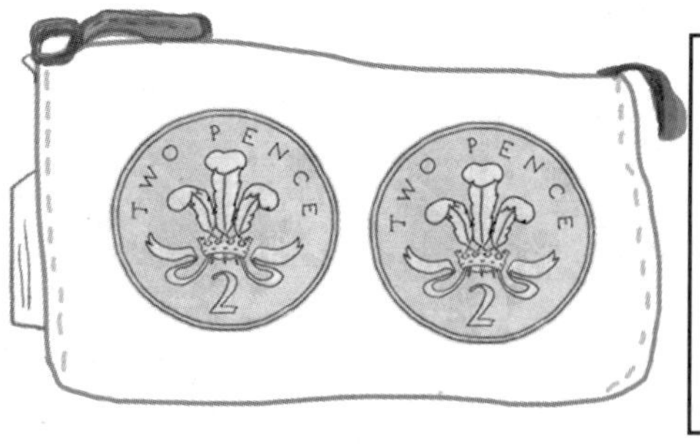

Teacher's notes

Children look at the coins in each purse and draw the number of 1p coins needed to make the same amount.
Allow the children to use 1p coins if necessary.

Name: _____ Date: _____

Coins and notes

Know the value of different coins and notes

You will need:
• 10p and
  £1 coins

Draw the number of 10p coins you would need:

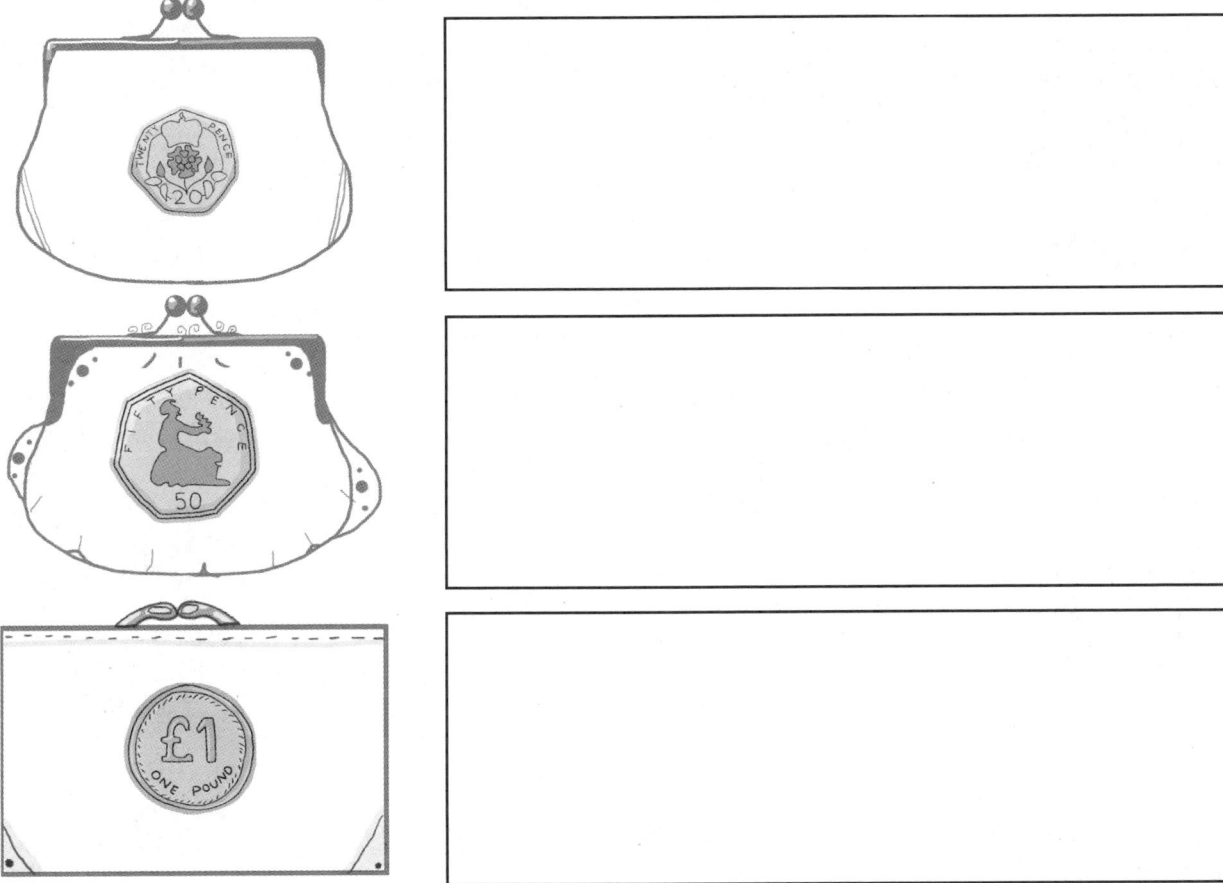

Draw the number of £1 coins you would need:

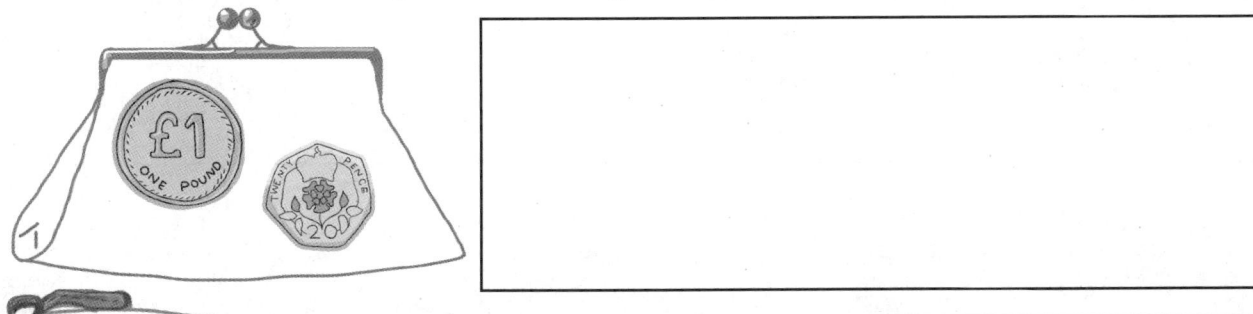

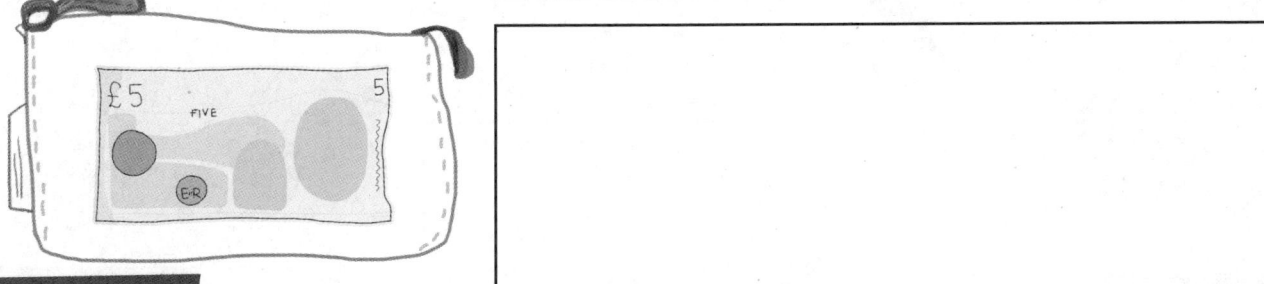

Teacher's notes

Children look at each amount of money and draw coins in the box to show the equivalent value. Allow the children to use 10p and £1 coins if necessary.

Name: _____ Date: _____

Money problems

Solve problems about money

☐ + ☐ = ☐

☐ + ☐ = ☐

 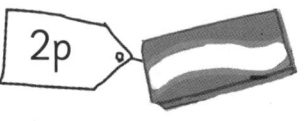 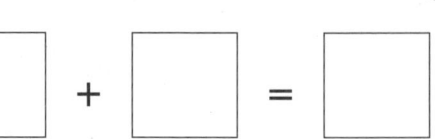    

☐ + ☐ = ☐

  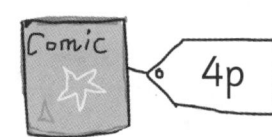    

☐ + ☐ = ☐

Teacher's notes

Children write the number sentence to show the total cost for each child's items. Then they circle the coins needed to pay for each pair of items. Note that each group of coins contains two or three 'extra' coins.

Name: _____ Date: _____

Ordering owls

Order numbers to 20

You will need:
- scissors
- glue

Teacher's notes

Children cut out the missing numbers from the bottom of the sheet. They then glue them in the correct positions so that each set of three numbers is in order, smallest to largest.

Name: _____ Date: _____

Odds and evens gardens

Know odd and even numbers to 10

You will need:
- scissors
- glue

odds

evens

Teacher's notes

Children cut out the flowers from the bottom of the sheet and glue them in the correct garden: odds or evens. In each garden they draw one more flower that belongs there.

Name: _____ Date: _____

Wallpaper patterns

Make repeating patterns

You will need:
- scissors
- glue

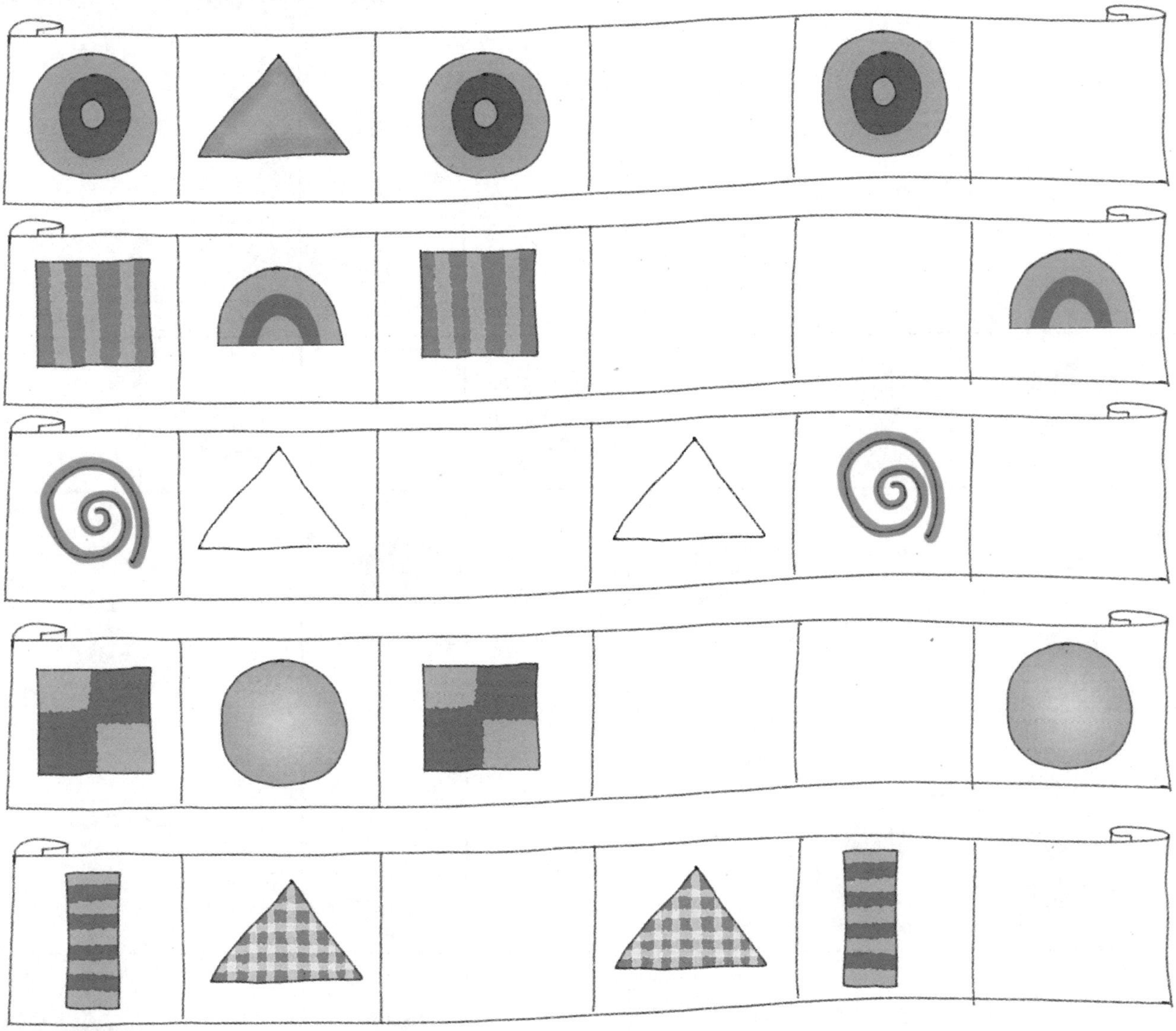

Teacher's notes

Children cut out the shapes from the bottom of the sheet. They then glue them in the correct places to complete each repeating wallpaper border pattern.

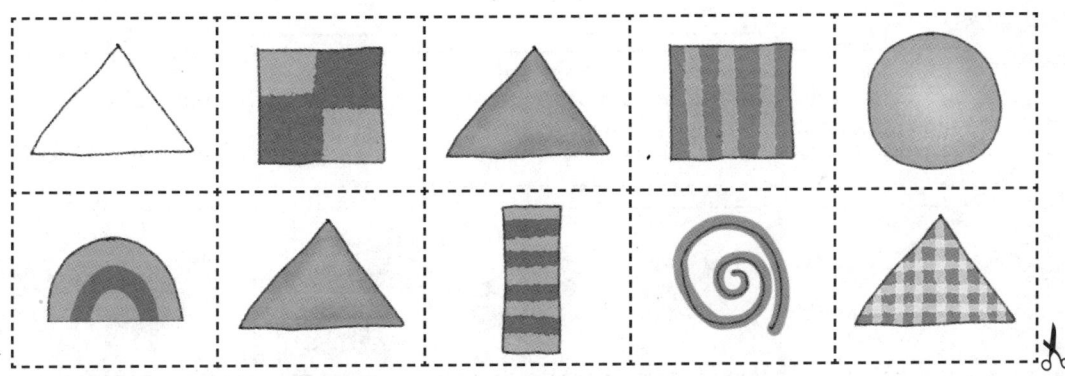

Name: _____ **Date:** _____

Pathway patterns

Make repeating patterns

You will need:
- scissors
- glue

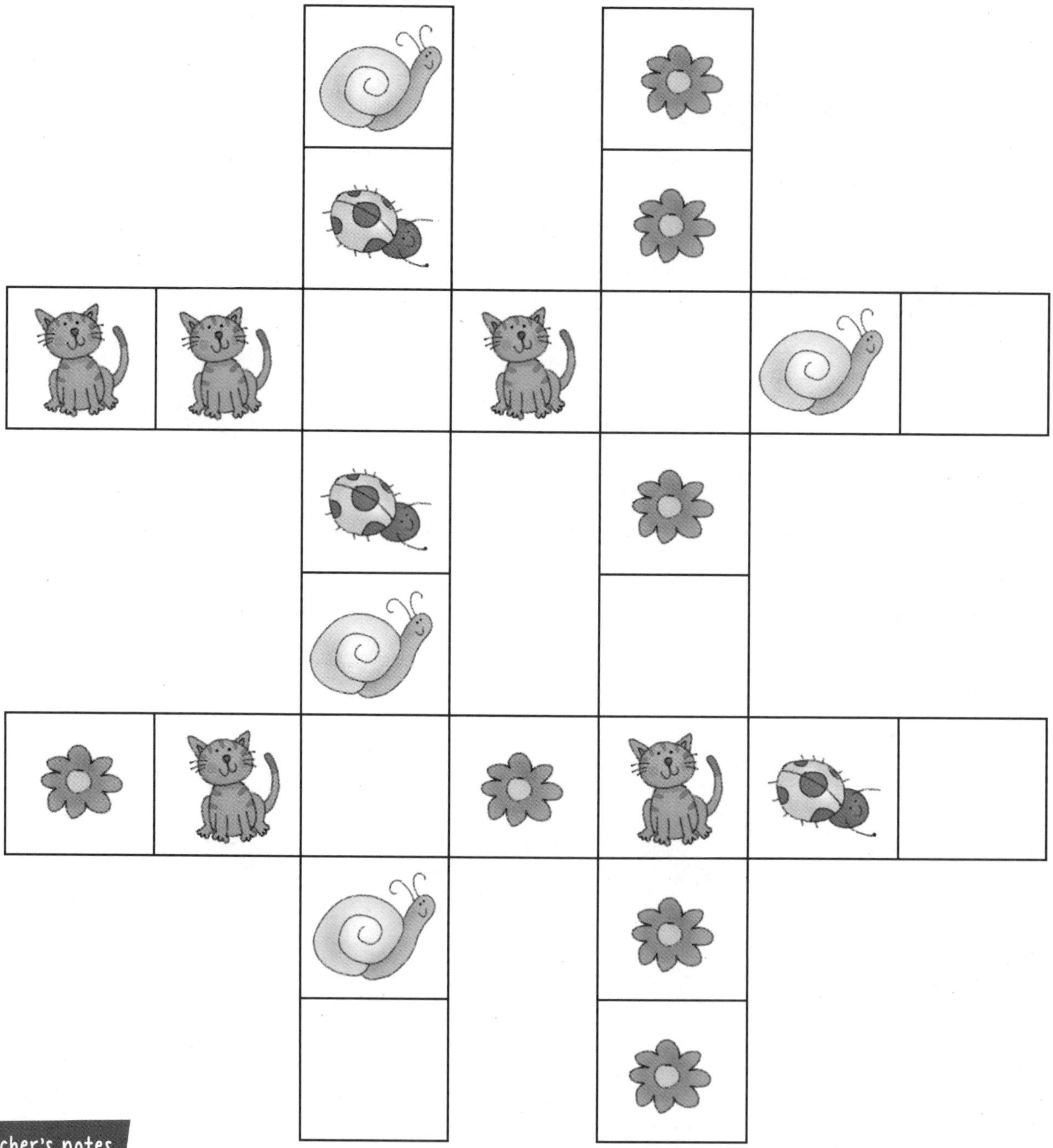

Teacher's notes

Children cut out the pictures from the bottom of the sheet. They then glue them in the correct spaces to complete the repeating pattern on each pathway.

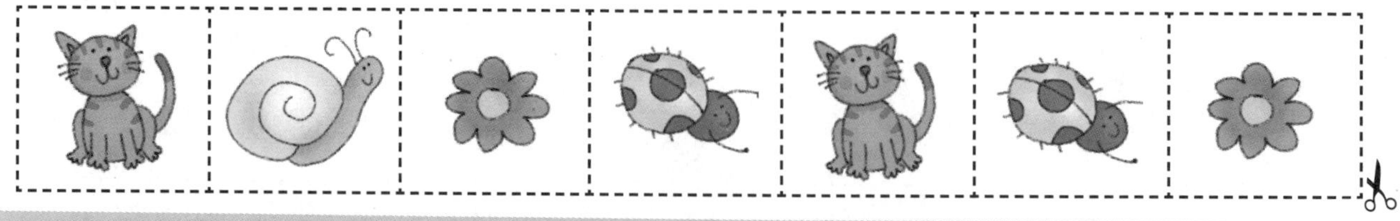

     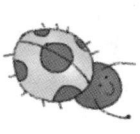 

Name: _____ Date: _____

oin collections

Solve problems about money

You will need:
- scissors
- glue

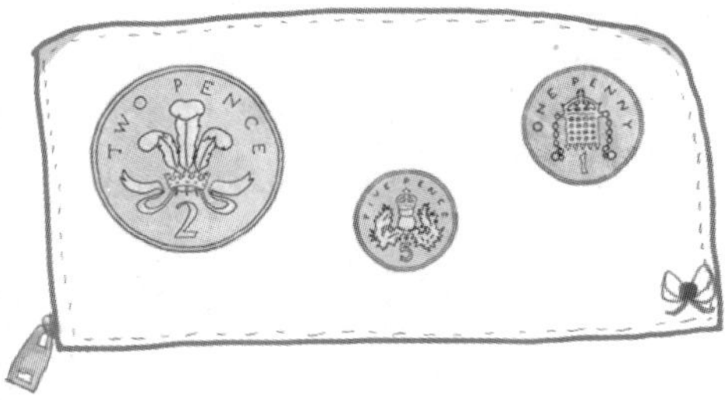

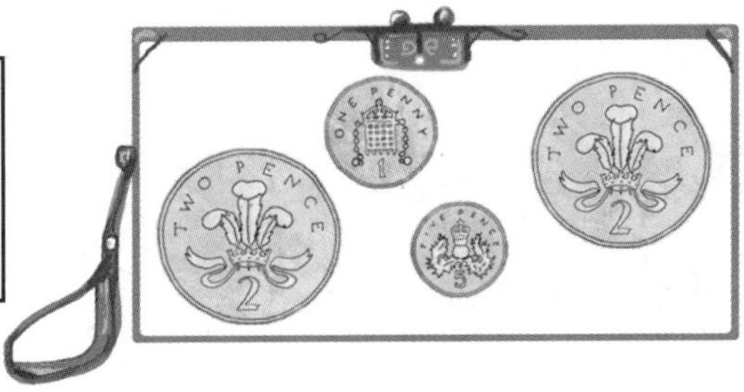

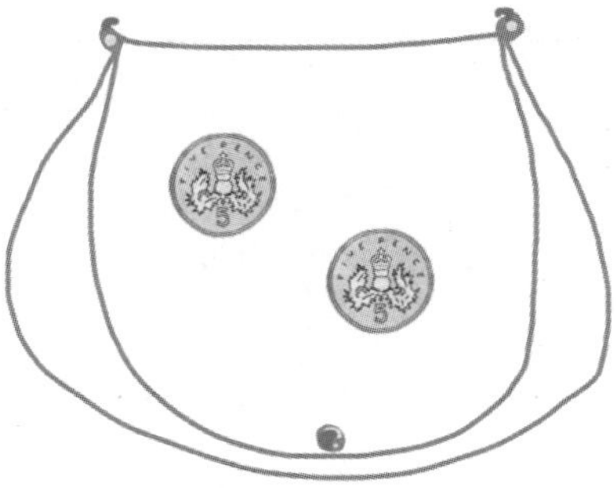

Teacher's notes

Children cut out the amounts of money from the bottom of the sheet. They find the total amount of money in each purse and glue the correct totals in the spaces provided.

| 7p | 10p | 6p | 8p | 5p | 10p | 7p | 9p |

Name: _____ Date: _____

Making money

Solve problems involving money

Make 5p.
Use 3 coins.

Make 7p.
Use 2 coins.

Make 6p.
Use 3 coins.

Make 10p.
Use 5 coins.

Make 5p.
Use the fewest coins.

Teacher's notes

Children draw the given number of coins to match the total.

Name: _____ Date: _____

What can I buy?

Solve money problems

Ali buys:

[ ] p + [ ] p = 15p

Sarah buys:

[ ] p + [ ] p = 15p

Lucy buys:

[ ] p + [ ] p = 15p

Patrick buys:

[ ] p + [ ] p = 15p

Teacher's notes

Children cut out the items from the bottom of the sheet and pair them so that each pair totals 15p. They give each character a pair of items, glue them into place and complete the addition calculation.

8p	6p	7p	10p	4p	11p	5p	9p

Name: _____ Date: _____

How much left?
Solve money problems

You will need:
- scissors
- glue

Zac has 15p. He buys: 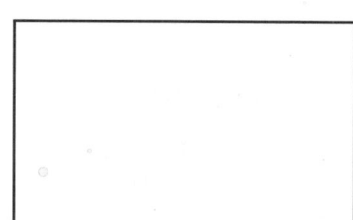 6p

☐ p – ☐ p = ☐ p

Kaya has 15p. She buys:  7p

☐ p – ☐ p = ☐ p

Matty has 15p. He buys: 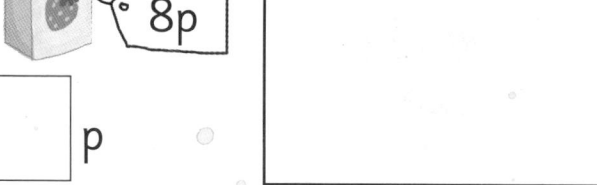 8p

☐ p – ☐ p = ☐ p

Mia has 15p. She buys:  9p

☐ p – ☐ p = ☐ p

Teacher's notes

Children complete each subtraction calculation, if necessary using the row of pennies to help them work out how much each character will have left. They then cut out the groups of coins from the bottom of the sheet and glue them in place to show what the amount left might look like.

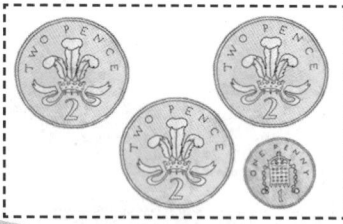     

Name: _____ Date: _____

Who has which shape?

Solve problems about 3-D shapes

You will need:
- red, orange, yellow, green, blue and purple coloured pencils
- 3-D shapes – cuboid, cube, pyramid, sphere, cylinder, cone

Dexter, Madison and Ying each have a different 3-D shape. Who has which shape and what colour is it?

- The shapes are a cuboid, a sphere and a pyramid.
- The colours are green, red and yellow.
- Madison's shape is a pyramid. It is not yellow.
- Dexter's shape is red. It is not a cuboid.

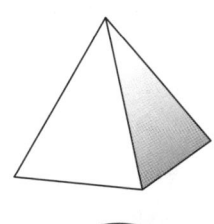

Dexter Madison Ying

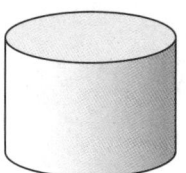

Naisha Sam Rosie

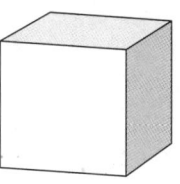

Naisha, Sam and Rosie each have a different 3-D shape. Who has which shape and what colour is it?

- The shapes are a cube, cone and cylinder.
- Naisha's shape is purple.
- The colours are purple, blue and orange.
- Rosie's shape is a cylinder. It is not orange.
- Sam's shape is not a cone.

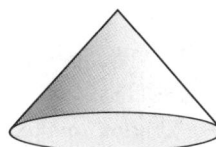

Teacher's notes

Children use the clues to identify which child has which 3-D shape and what colour it would be. They draw a line to join each child to their shape and then colour the shape. Provide reading support and prompt children, if necessary, to read each set of four clues and pick out the coloured pencils and 3-D shapes involved.

Name: _____ Date: _____

3-D shape models

Name and make models of 3-D shapes

You will need:
- 3-D shapes – cuboid, cube, pyramid, sphere, cylinder, cone
- putty
- scissors

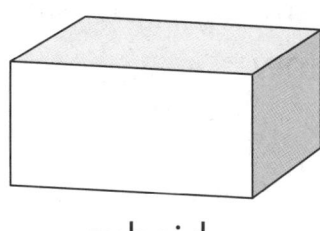

cuboid

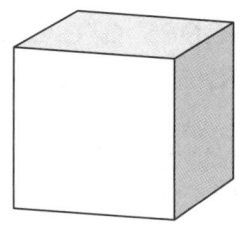

cube

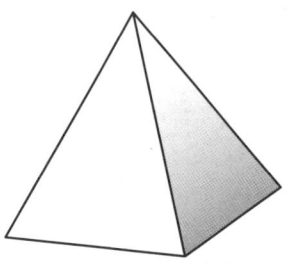

pyramid

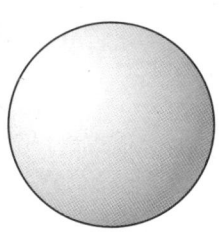

sphere

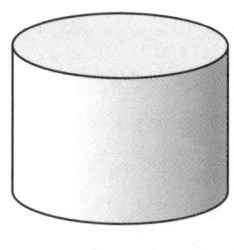

cylinder

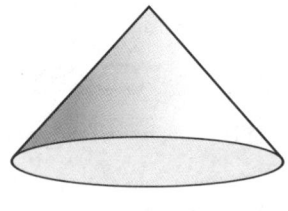

cone

Teacher's notes

Children make putty models using a set of 3-D shapes and the shapes on this sheet to guide them. They cut out the shape names from the bottom of the sheet and use them to label their models. They photograph their labelled model alongside the corresponding 3-D shape, print the photograph and stick it on the back of this page.

cube	sphere	cuboid
cylinder	pyramid	cone

Name: _____ Date: _____

3-D shapes and 2-D shapes

Know and name 3-D shapes

You will need:
- 3-D shapes –
  cuboid, cube,
  pyramid, sphere,
  cylinder, cone

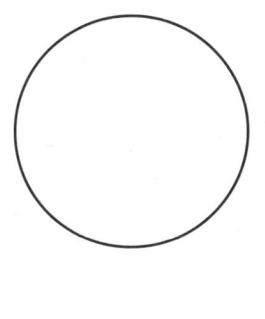

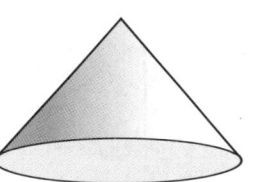

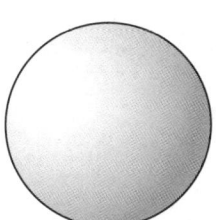

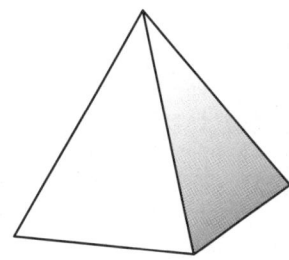

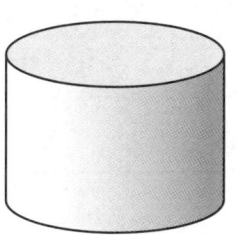

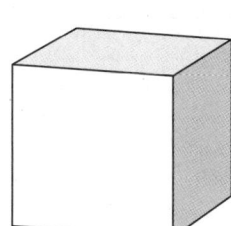

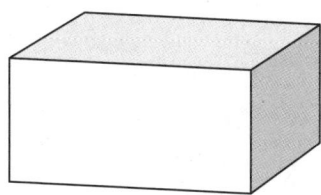

Teacher's notes

For each 3-D shape, children draw a line from the 3-D shape picture to any of the 2-D shapes they can see as they turn the 3-D shape around. Note that the pyramid pictured here is of a square-based pyramid. You may or may not also want to include a triangular-based pyramid and discuss with the children the similarities and difference between these two types of pyramid.

Name: _____ Date: _____

2-D and 3-D shapes

Know 2-D and 3-D shapes

You will need:
- red and yellow coloured pencils
- 2-D and 3-D shapes

2-D shapes

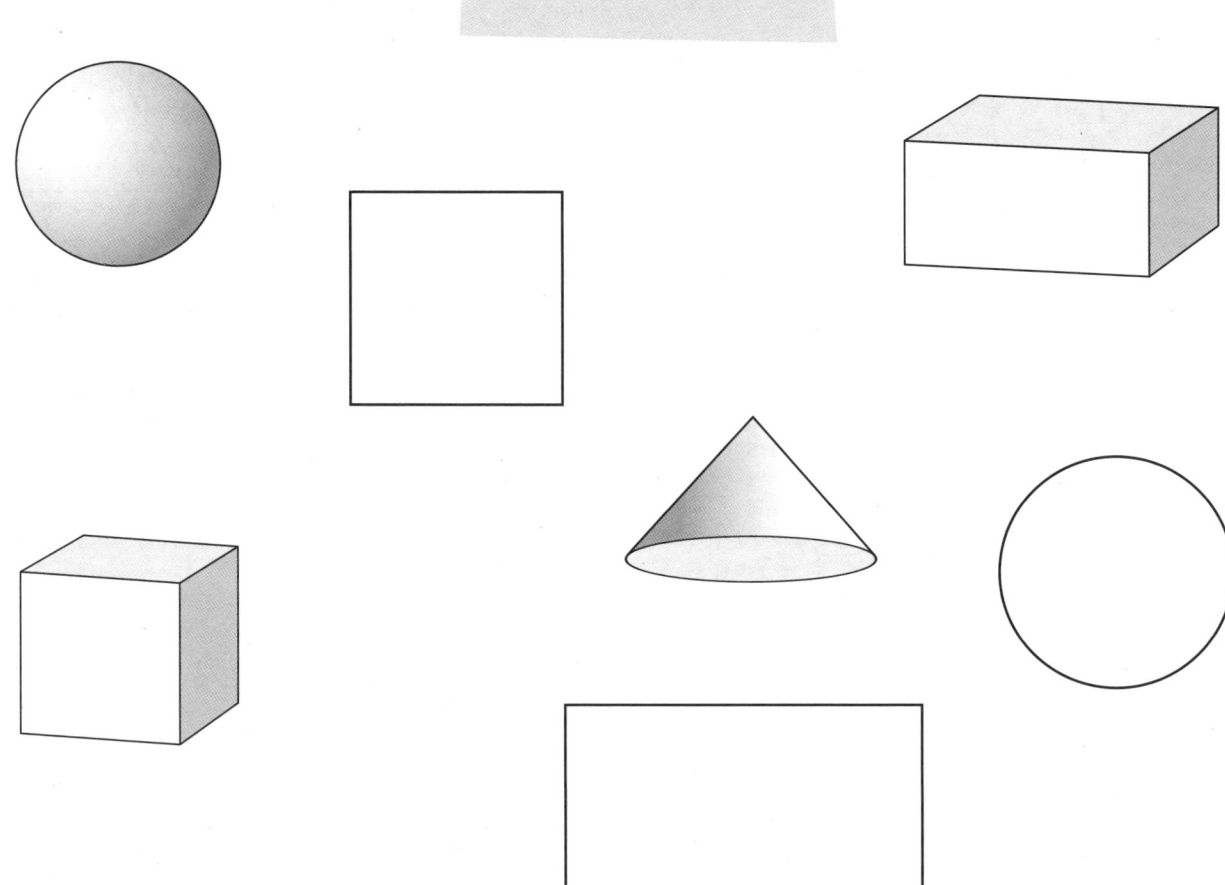

3-D shapes

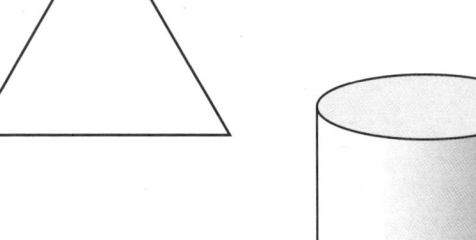

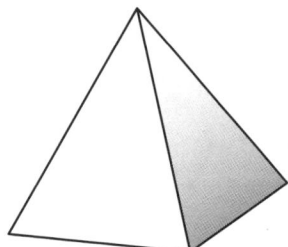

Teacher's notes

Children colour the 2-D shapes red and the 3-D shapes yellow. They then draw a line from each shape to the correct label.

Name: _____ Date: _____

Bug trail 2s

Count in 2s

You will need:
- scissors
- glue

 0	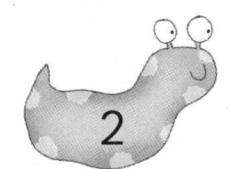 2		 6	 8
	 8	 10	 12	
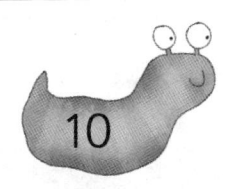 10		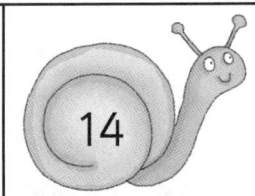 14	 16	
 16	 18		 22	 24
	 24	 26		 30

Teacher's notes

Children cut out the bugs at the bottom of the sheet and, counting in twos, glue each one in the correct place in a row.

 22	4	 28	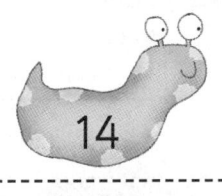 14
12	 20	6	18

Name: _____ Date: _____

Patterns of 5s

Count in 5s

You will need:
- scissors
- glue

| 15 | 20 | | | 35 |

| 5 | | 15 | | 25 |

| 30 | | 40 | | 50 |

Teacher's notes

Children cut out the multiples of five at the bottom of the sheet and glue them onto the rockets in order, 0–50. They then complete each row of stars by writing the missing multiples of five in the spaces.

| 25 | 15 | 0 | 45 | 35 | 5 | 20 | 50 | 10 | 30 | 40 |

Name: _____ Date: _____

Tomato ketchup 10s

Count in 10s

[ ] [ ] [ ] [ ] [ ] [ ] [ ] [ ] [ ] [ ] [ ]

Row 1: 20 | [ ] | [ ] | 50

Row 2: 40 | 50 | [ ] | [ ]

Row 3: 70 | [ ] | 90 | [ ]

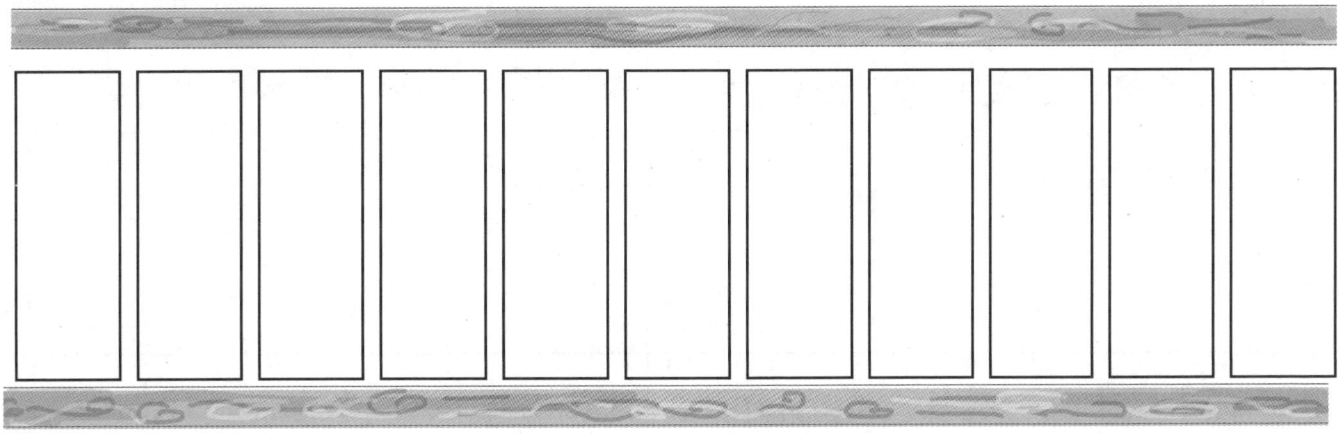

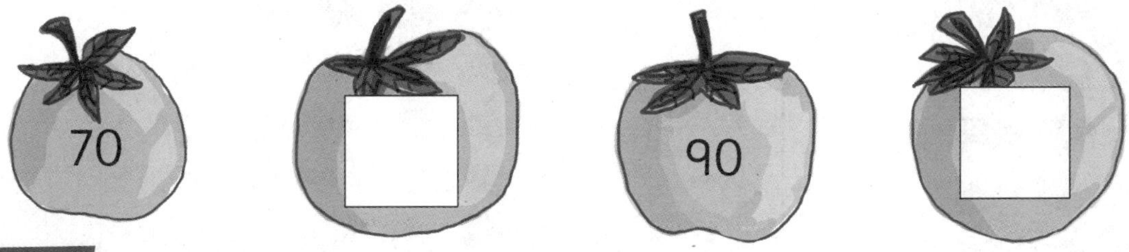

Teacher's notes

Children cut out the multiples of ten at the bottom of the sheet and glue them onto the shelf in order,
0–100. They then complete each row of tomatoes by writing the missing multiples of ten in the spaces.

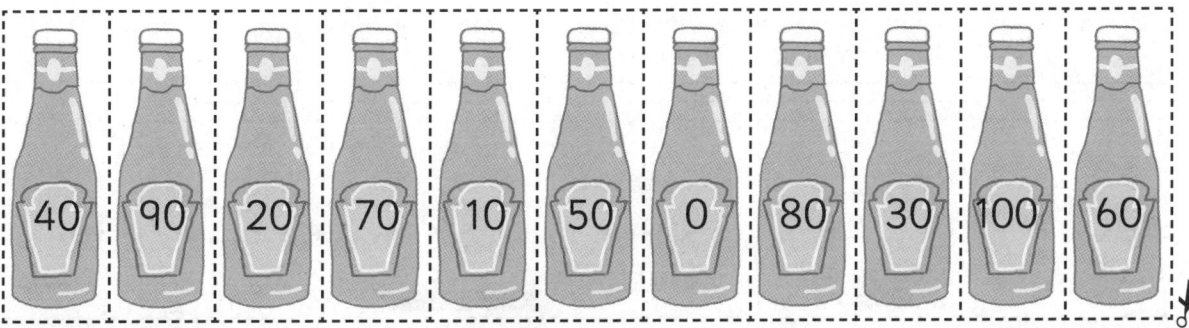

40 | 90 | 20 | 70 | 10 | 50 | 0 | 80 | 30 | 100 | 60

Name: _____ Date: _____

All at sea

Use arrays to count in 2s, 5s and 10s

You will need:
- scissors
- glue

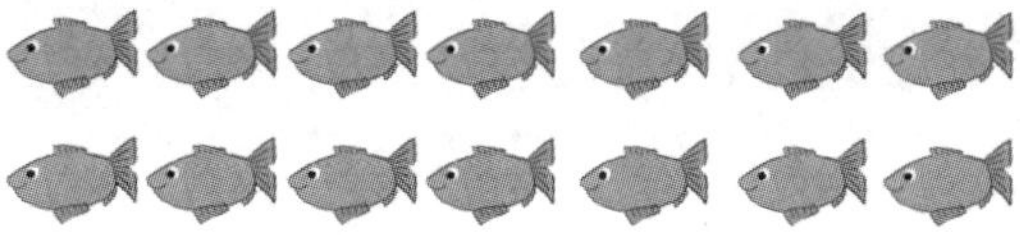

Count in 2s. ☐

Count in 2s. ☐

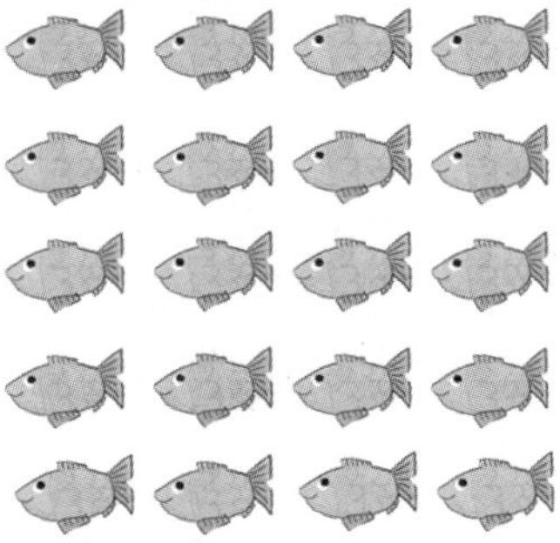

Count in 5s.

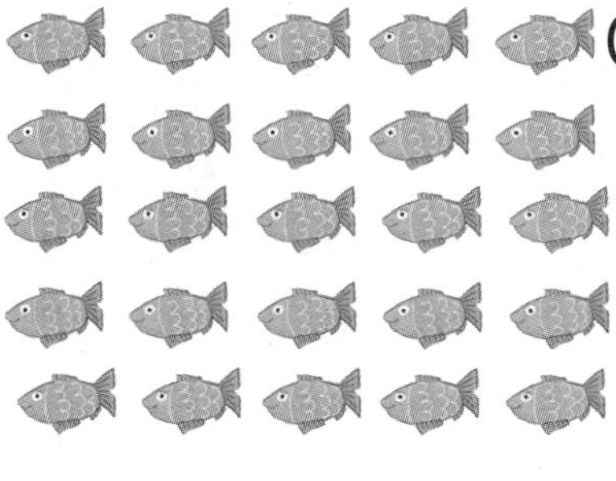

Count in 5s. ☐

Count in 5s. ☐

Count in 10s. ☐

Count in 5s or 10s. ☐

Teacher's notes

Children cut out the boats at the bottom of the sheet. They count the fish in each shoal in twos, fives or tens, and glue the boat with the correct total next to it.

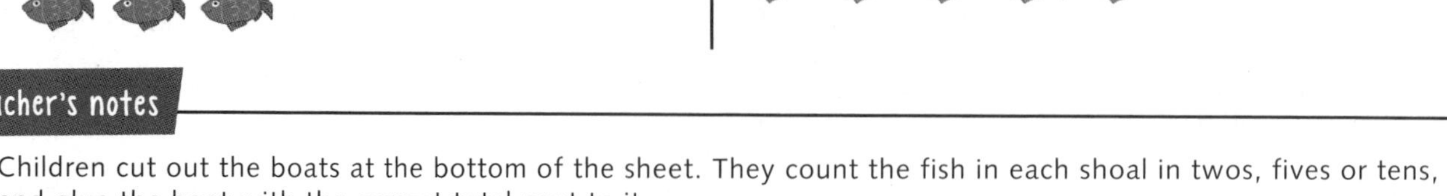

 14
 25
 30
 18
 20
 50

Name: _____ Date: _____

low many bugs?

Find a total by counting sets of 2, 5 or 10

You will need:
- scissors
- glue

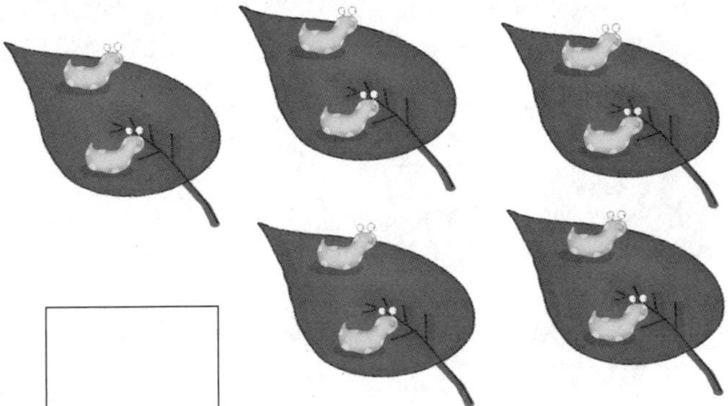

☐ bugs altogether

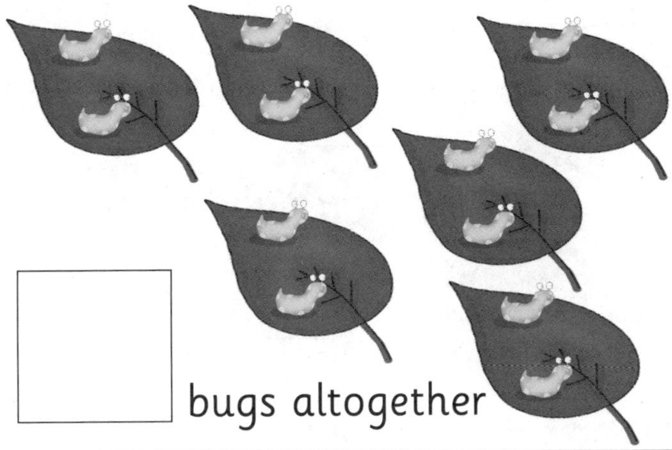

☐ bugs altogether

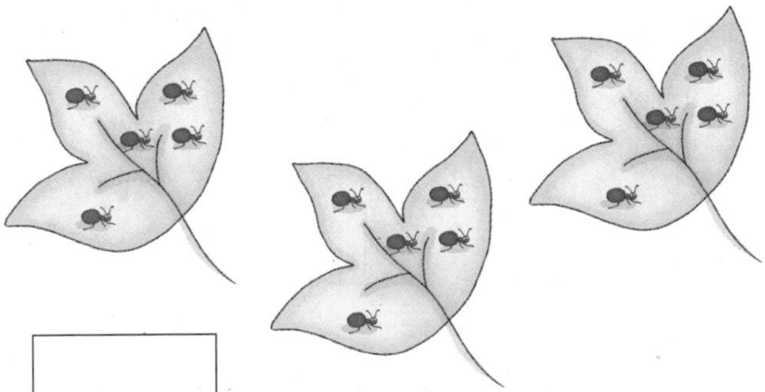

☐ bugs altogether

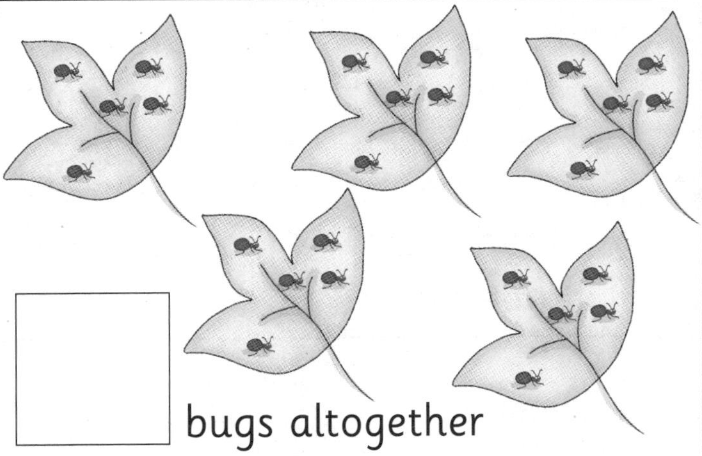

☐ bugs altogether

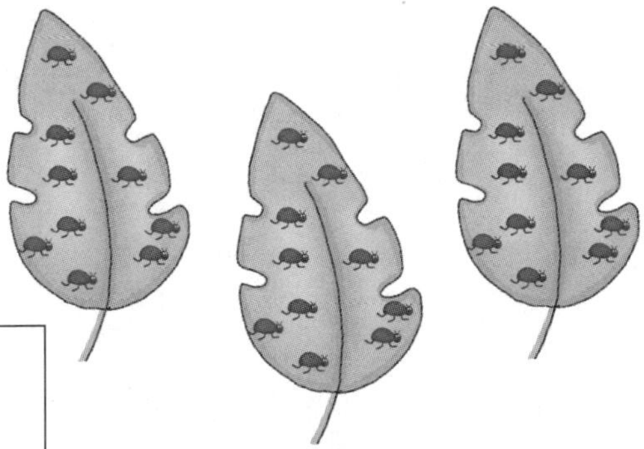

☐ bugs altogether

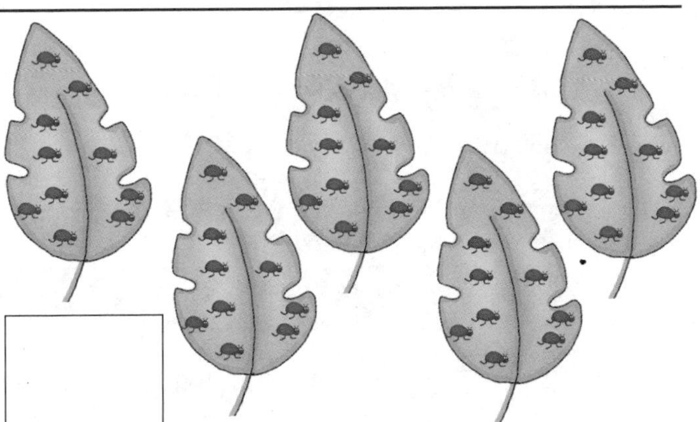

☐ bugs altogether

Teacher's notes

Children cut out the numbers at the bottom of the sheet. They count in twos, fives or tens to find out how many bugs are in each section and glue the correct number into the space.

| 15 | 30 | 10 | 50 | 25 | 12 |

Name: _____ Date: _____

Shopping problems

Find a total by counting sets of 2, 5 or 10

You will need:
• coloured pencils

There are ☐ socks in a pair.

Khalid buys ☐ pairs.

Khalid buys ☐ socks altogether.

There are ☐ pens in a pack.

Thea buys ☐ packs.

Thea buys ☐ pens altogether.

There are ☐ biscuits in a packet.

Leon buys ☐ packets.

Leon buys ☐ biscuits altogether.

Now make up your own problem about sets of 2, 5 or 10.

Teacher's notes

Children count the number of items in each lot (two, five or ten) and the number of sets to find out how many of each item the characters buy. They then make up their own problem involving sets of two, five or ten.

Name: _____   Date: _____

Sharing spots

Share objects into equal groups

There are [ ] spots on each bug.

There are [ ] spots on each bug.

There are [ ] spots on each bug.

There are [ ] spots on each bug.

There are [ ] spots on each bug.

There are [ ] spots on each bug.

Teacher's notes

Children count the number of spots and share them equally between the bugs by drawing them on. They then write how many spots there are on each bug.

Name: _____ Date: _____

Share with friends

Share objects into equal groups

You will need:
• counting objects,
  such as counters
  or beads

[ ] shared between [ ]

is [ ] each.

[ ] shared between [ ]

is [ ] each.

[ ] shared between [ ]

is [ ] each.

[ ] shared between [ ]

is [ ] each.

Teacher's notes

Children count the number of objects and share them equally between the people shown, using counting objects to help if needed. They then complete the sharing sentence.

Name: _____ Date: _____

Lightest to heaviest

Compare weights

 ☐    ☐    ☐

 ☐    ☐    ☐

 ☐   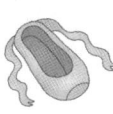 ☐    ☐

 ☐    ☐   ☐

 ☐    ☐    ☐

 ☐    ☐    ☐

☐    ☐    ☐    ☐    ☐

Name: _____ **Date:** _____

Comparing mass

Understand what a balance shows

Teacher's notes

For the first four pictures, children write 'heavier', 'lighter' or 'equal' under each side of the balance. For the last two pictures, they draw a suitable object in each pan.

Name: _____ Date: _____

How many to balance?

Weigh objects

You will need:
• balance
• objects to weigh
• set of cubes, bricks or blocks

a book

a pen

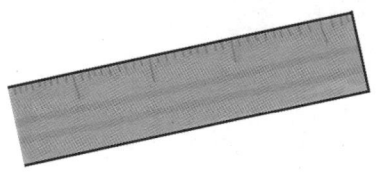

a ruler

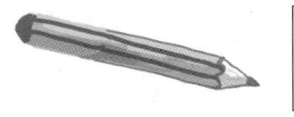

a pencil

The heaviest object is the _____ .

The lightest object is the _____ .

Teacher's notes

Children use a balance and uniform cubes, bricks or blocks to find the weight of each object and record it in the box. Then they complete the sentences.

Name: _____ Date: _____

Reading scales

Weigh objects

pineapple: ⬜ kilograms

cat: ⬜ kilograms

melon: ⬜ kilograms

book: ⬜ kilograms

The heaviest object is the _____ .

The lightest object is the _____ .

Teacher's notes

Children write down how many kilograms each object weighs. Then they complete the sentences.

Name: _____   Date: _____

Storeys of 10

Know pairs of numbers that add up to 10

You will need:
• coloured pencils

Teacher's notes

Children draw faces at each pair of windows to total ten.

Name: _____ Date: _____

Pencil pot problems

Use doubles to work out addition calculations

5 + 6

5 + 5 + 1

10 + 1

5 + 6 =

5 + 8

5 + +

10 +

+ =

5 + 7

+ +

+

+ =

5 + 9

+ +

+

+ =

Name: _____   Date: _____

Calculation rescue

- Know addition facts to 10
- Use addition facts to find subtraction facts

| 6 | 7 | 8 | 9 | 10 |

$5 + 2$ $6 + 4$ $4 + 2$ $7 + 1$ $9 + 0$

$10 - 4 = 6$ $6 - 2 = 4$ $7 - 2 = 5$ $9 - 0 = 9$ $8 - 1 = 7$

Teacher's notes

Children first draw a line to join the answer on each knight's shield to the flag showing the matching addition calculation. Then they draw a line from each flag to the turret showing the related subtraction fact.

Name: _____ Date: _____

Bead addition and subtraction

- Know subtraction facts to 10
- Use addition facts to find subtraction facts

☐ + ☐ = ☐

☐ − ☐ = ☐

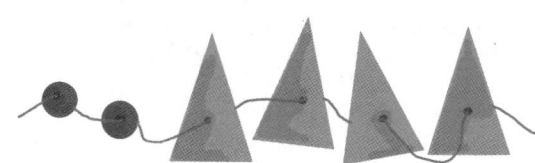

☐ + ☐ = ☐

☐ − ☐ = ☐

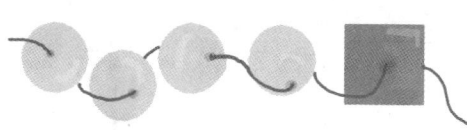

☐ + ☐ = ☐

☐ − ☐ = ☐

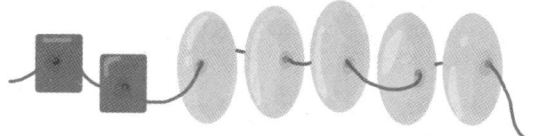

☐ + ☐ = ☐

☐ − ☐ = ☐

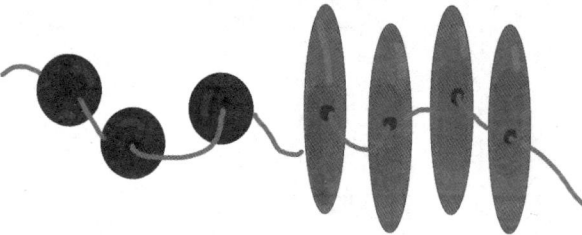

☐ + ☐ = ☐

☐ − ☐ = ☐

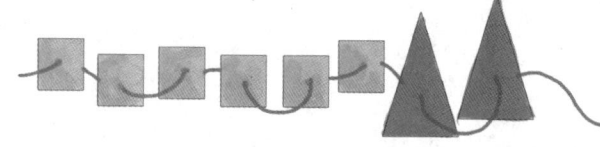

☐ + ☐ = ☐

☐ − ☐ = ☐

Teacher's notes

Children count the number of beads of each shape, write the numbers in the boxes and complete the addition calculation. They use the same beads and numbers to write a related subtraction calculation.

Name: _____ Date: _____

pple basket addition

Addition as counting on

0 1 2 3 4 5 6 7 8 9 10 11 12 13 14 15 16 17 18 19 20

7 + ☐ = ☐

9 + ☐ = ☐

7 + ☐ = ☐

10 + ☐ = ☐

9 + ☐ = ☐

Teacher's notes

Children use each pair of numbers to write an addition calculation, using the number track to help them work out the answer if necessary.

Name: _____ Date: _____

Sea subtraction

Subtraction as counting back

0 1 2 3 4 5 6 7 8 9 10 11 12 13 14 15

7 **10** | **5** **11**

[10] (−) [7] ( ) [ ] | [ ] ( ) [ ] ( ) [ ]

12 **4** | **6** **13**

[ ] ( ) [ ] ( ) [ ] | [ ] ( ) [ ] ( ) [ ]

8 **14** | **15** **4**

[ ] ( ) [ ] ( ) [ ] | [ ] ( ) [ ] ( ) [ ]

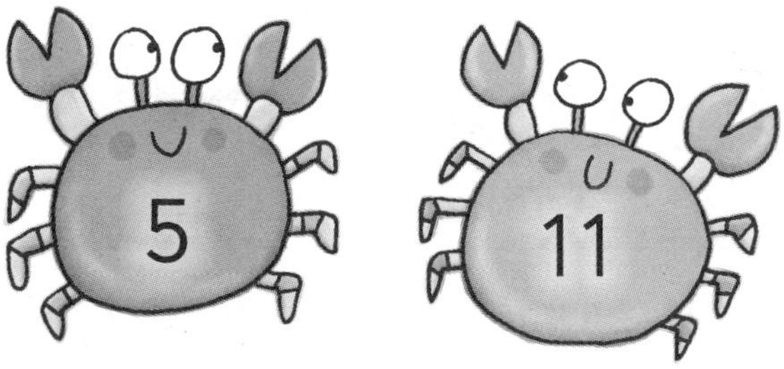

Teacher's notes

Children use each pair of numbers to write a subtraction calculation, using the number track to help them work out the answer if necessary. Remind the children of the need to put the larger number first.

Name: _____ Date: _____

Picnic problems

Solve addition and subtraction missing number problems

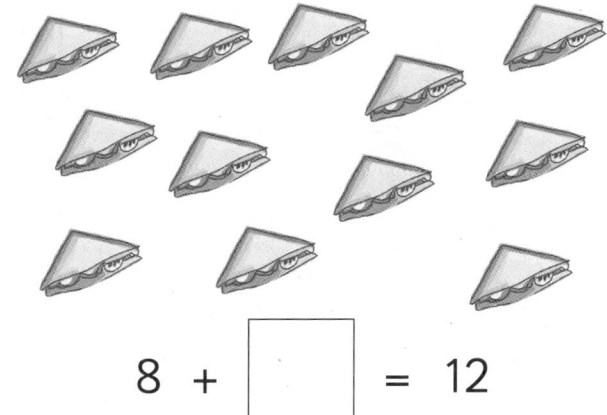

8 + ☐ = 12

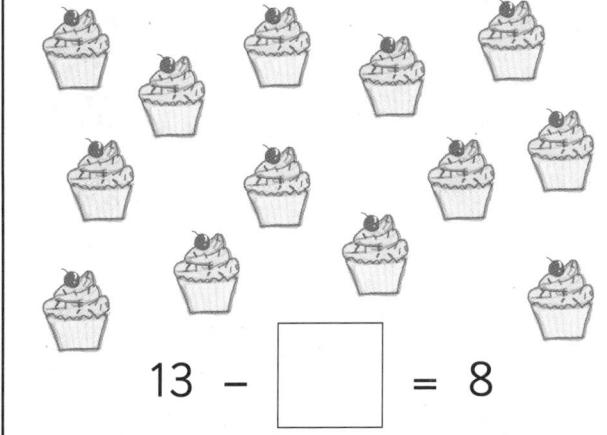

13 – ☐ = 8

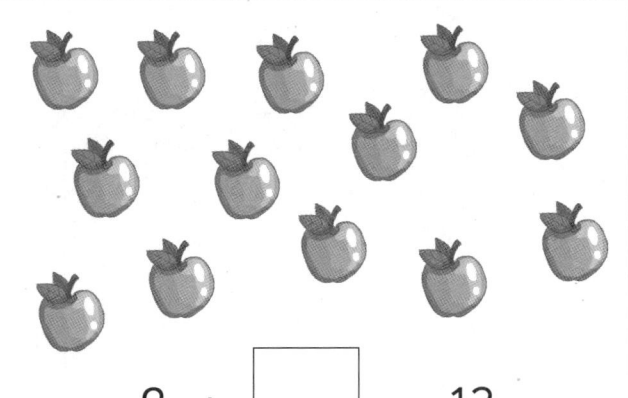

9 + ☐ = 13

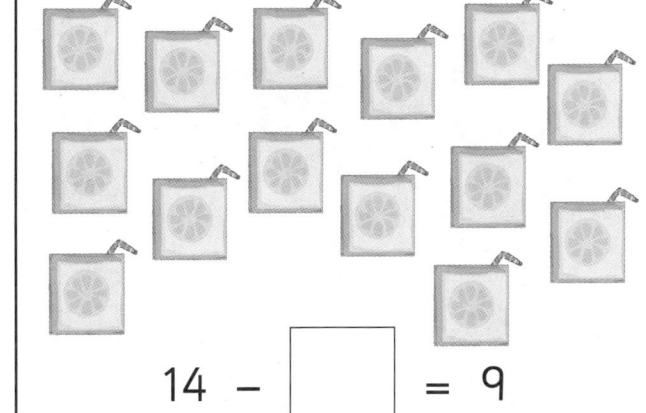

14 – ☐ = 9

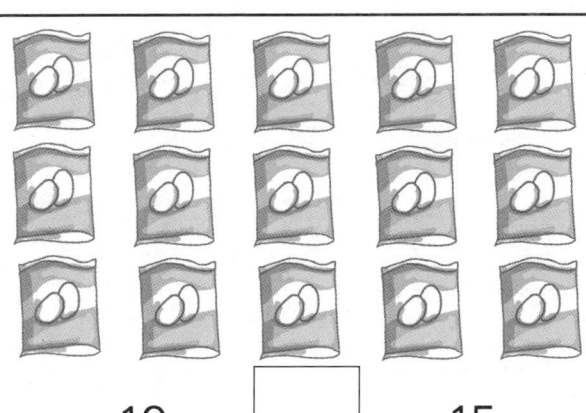

10 + ☐ = 15

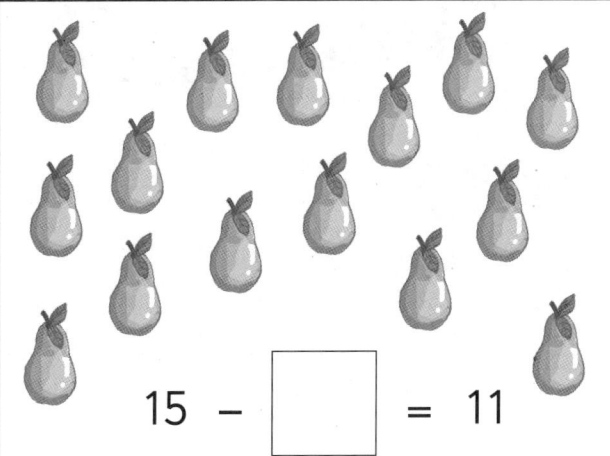

15 – ☐ = 11

Teacher's notes

Children use the number track and picnic items to find the missing number in each addition or subtraction calculation.

Name: _____ Date: _____

Flag facts

Find patterns in addition and subtraction calculations

You will need:
• scissors
• glue

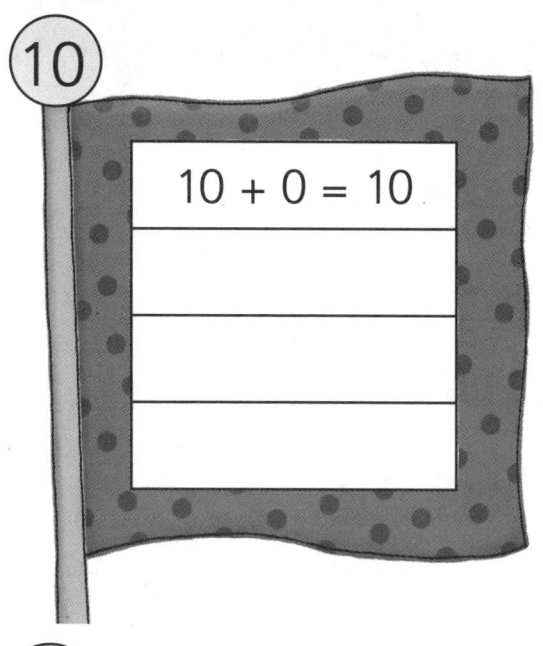

10

10 + 0 = 10

10

10 − 0 = 10

11

11 + 0 = 11

11

11 − 0 = 11

Teacher's notes

Children cut out the number facts at the bottom of the sheet and sort them into addition and subtraction sets for 10 and 11. They glue each set of facts on the appropriate flag, in order.

10 − 1 = 9	9 + 1 = 10	11 − 2 = 9	9 + 2 = 11
11 − 1 = 10	10 − 2 = 8	8 + 3 = 11	8 + 2 = 10
7 + 3 = 10	10 + 1 = 11	10 − 3 = 7	11 − 3 = 8

Name: _____ Date: _____

ays and months

Order the days of the week and months of the year

Sunday

_____

_____

_____

_____

_____

_____

comes before   comes after

 March _____ February

 January _____ December

 November _____ December

 August _____ September

_____ and July

 October _____ November

_____ and September

Teacher's notes

At the top of the sheet, children write the missing days of the week in the spaces provided. In the bottom section, they write the phrases 'comes before' or 'comes after' between each pair of months to indicate the correct order of the months.

Name: ______________________ Date: ______________

Sequencing seasons

Order the seasons

You will need:
- scissors
- glue
- coloured pencils

winter

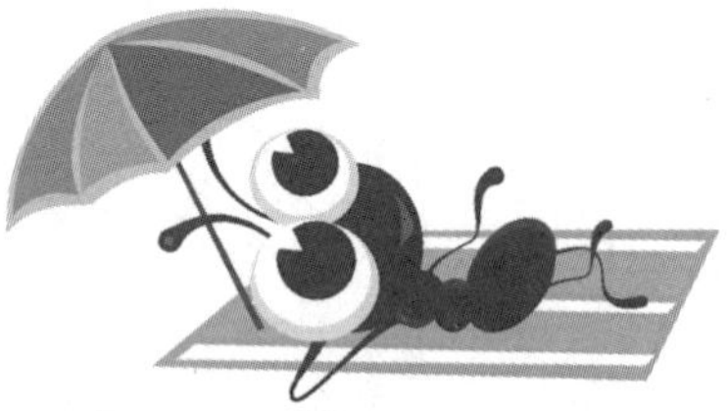

Teacher's notes

Children cut out the labels and glue them into the correct boxes to show the order of the seasons. They then draw a picture to show what each season is like.

summer	autumn	spring

Name: _____ Date: _____

elling the time

Read and show o'clock times

_____   _____   _____

_____

1 hour later

_____

1 hour earlier

_____

Teacher's notes

In the top row, children write the time underneath each clock face. In the bottom section, children write the time underneath the first clock in each pair. They then draw hands on the second clock face to show the time one hour later or one hour earlier.

Name: _____ Date: _____

More time

Read o'clock and half-past times

_____ _____ _____

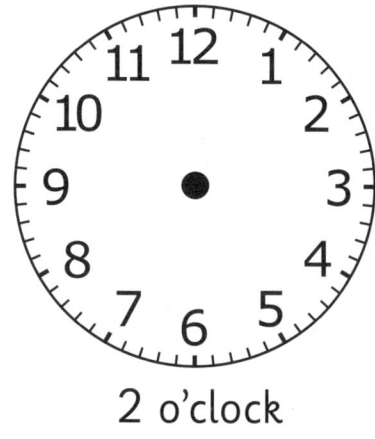 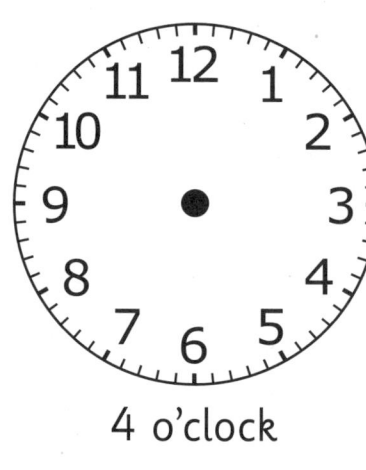 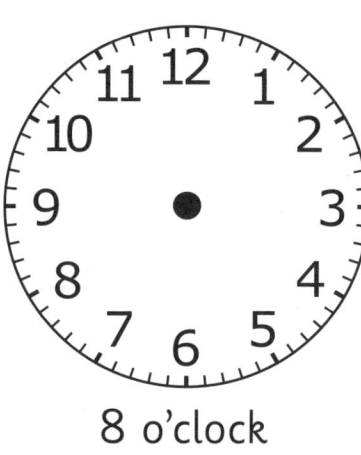

2 o'clock   4 o'clock   8 o'clock

                        half past 4   half past 8

_____

Teacher's notes

Children write the time underneath each clock face or draw hands on the clock face to show the time given.

Name: _____ Date: _____

Number names to 10

Read and write numbers in numerals and words

You will need:
• scissors
• glue

1		6	
2		7	
3		8	
4		9	
5		10	

Teacher's notes

Children cut out the sets at the bottom of the sheet. They count the number of bugs in each set and glue the number names next to the matching numerals.

 four	 seven	 one	 ten	 five
 two	 nine	 six	 three	 eight

Name: _____ Date: _____

Bowling scores

Find the number of 10s and 1s in 2-digit numbers

You will need:
• scissors
• glue

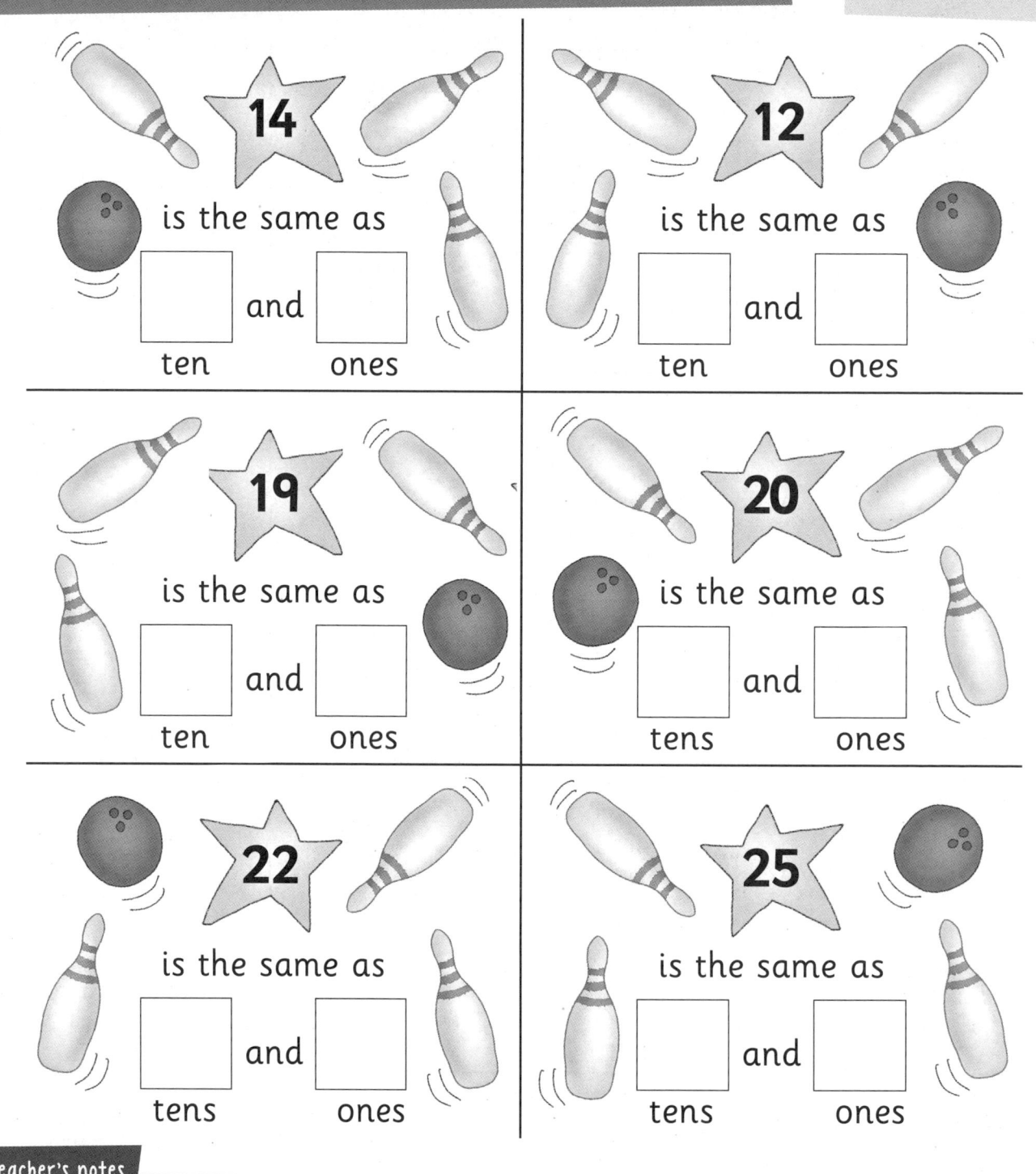

14 is the same as

☐ and ☐
ten   ones

12 is the same as

☐ and ☐
ten   ones

19 is the same as

☐ and ☐
ten   ones

20 is the same as

☐ and ☐
tens   ones

22 is the same as

☐ and ☐
tens   ones

25 is the same as

☐ and ☐
tens   ones

Teacher's notes

Children cut out the numbers at the bottom of the sheet and glue them in position to show the number of tens and ones in each bowling score.

| 2 | 1 | 2 | 4 | 2 | 1 | 1 | 2 | 2 | 0 | 5 | 9 |

Name: _____ Date: _____

Supermarket counting

Count a group of up to 20 objects

There are ☐ tomatoes.

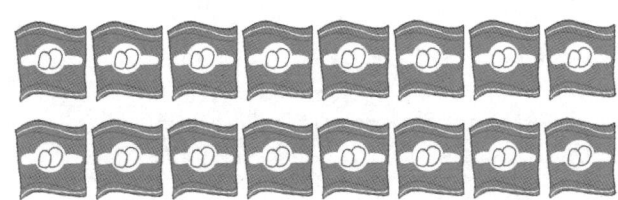

There are ☐ packets.

There are ☐ chillies.

There are ☐ tins.

There are ☐ bottles.

There are ☐ mangos.

 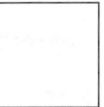

There are ☐ carrots.

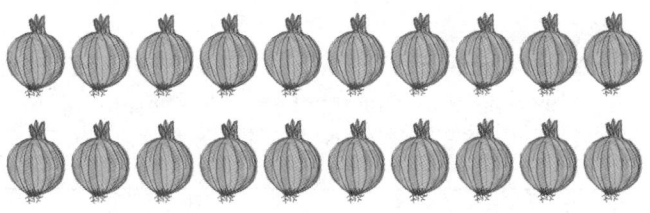

There are ☐ onions.

Teacher's notes

Children count and write the number of items in each set.

Name: _____ Date: _____

Multiples mix-up

Know multiples of 2, 5 and 10

You will need:
- scissors
- glue

These numbers are multiples of

 **2**

These numbers are multiples of

 **5**

These numbers are multiples of

10

These numbers are multiples of

2, 5, 10

| 70 | 10 | 35 | 100 | 14 | 45 | 50 | 22 |

Name: _____ Date: _____

Quick quarters

Find a quarter of a shape

You will need:
- coloured pencils

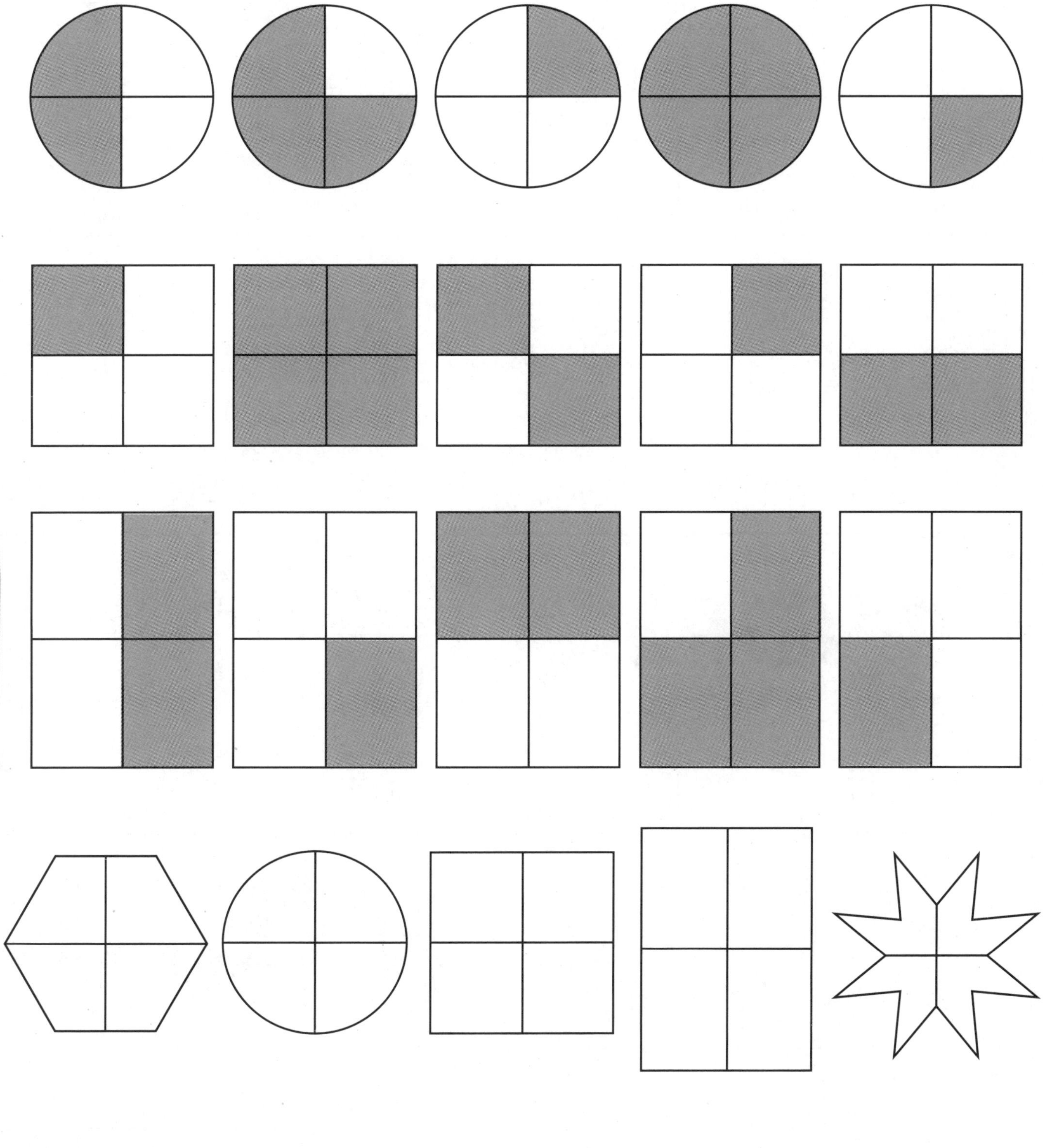

Teacher's notes

For the first three rows, children draw a ring around the shape in each row that shows one quarter shaded.
For the bottom row, children colour one quarter of each shape.

Name: _____ Date: _____

Quarter questions

Find a quarter of a set of objects

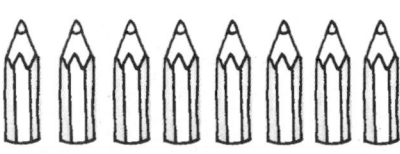

$\frac{1}{4}$ of  is  .

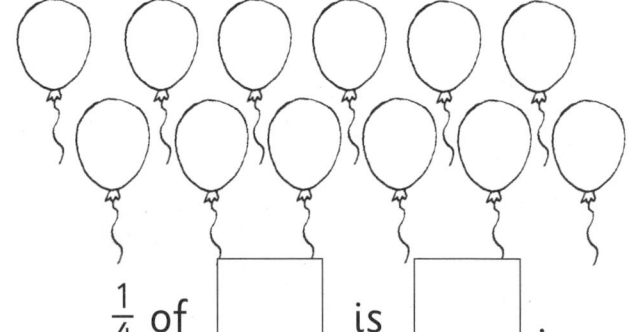

$\frac{1}{4}$ of ☐ is ☐ .

$\frac{1}{4}$ of  is  .

$\frac{1}{4}$ of ☐ is  .

$\frac{1}{4}$ of  is  .

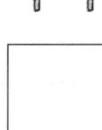

$\frac{1}{4}$ of ☐ is ☐ .

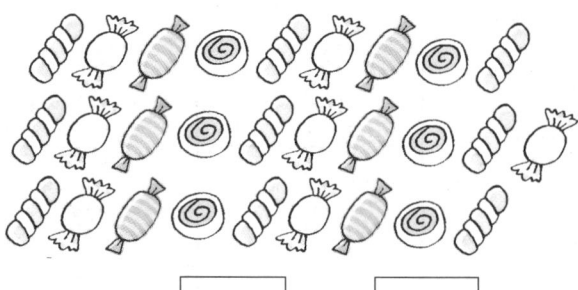

$\frac{1}{4}$ of  is  .

$\frac{1}{4}$ of ☐ is  .

Teacher's notes

Children count the number of objects in each set, colour one quarter and complete the sentence.

Name: _____ Date: _____

Cube tower quarters

Find a quarter of a length

You will need:
- coloured pencils

Teacher's notes

Children colour one quarter the number of cubes in each tower.

Name: _____ Date: _____

Picnic quarters

Combine quarters to make 1 whole

Each slice is $\frac{1}{4}$ of a pizza. How many pizzas have been shared?

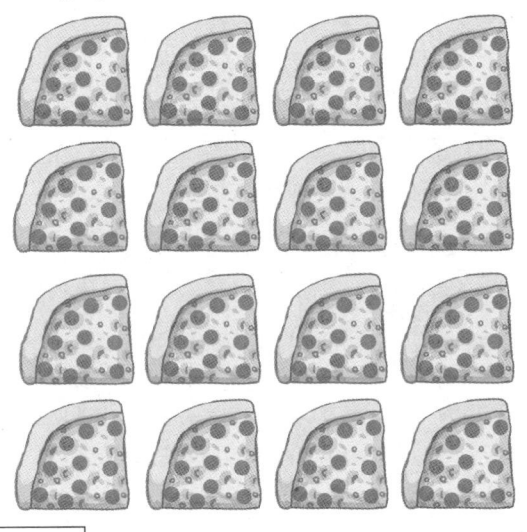

☐ pizzas altogether

Only 1 quarter of the packets of crisps are left. How many were there at the start of the picnic?

☐ packets altogether

1 quarter of the juice cartons are left. How many were there to start with?

☐ cartons altogether

Each slice is $\frac{1}{4}$ of a cake. How many cakes have been shared?

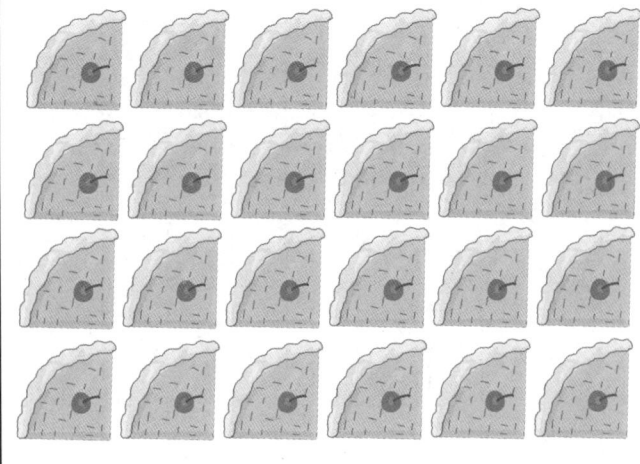

☐ cakes altogether

Teacher's notes

Children work out the amount of food and drink at a picnic. They combine quarters to make wholes and they work out how many there were of an item to start with when they know a quarter are left.

Name: _____ Date: _____

Full or empty?
Compare volumes

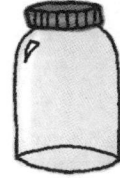

full

empty

Teacher's notes

Children look at each container and draw a line from the container to the matching label.

Name: _____   Date: _____

Comparing capacities
Compare non-standard measures

| spoon |  cup |  jug |  bigger spoon |  bucket |

holds least   **holds most**

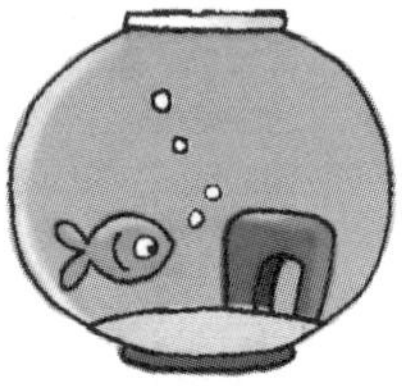

☐ cup
☐ bucket

☐ cup
☐ bucket

☐ cup
☐ bucket

☐ cup
☐ bucket

☐ cup
☐ bucket

☐ cup
☐ bucket

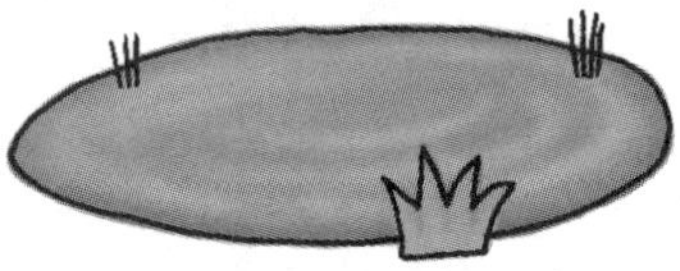

☐ cup
☐ bucket

☐ cup
☐ bucket

Teacher's notes

Children write the non-standard measures shown at the top of the sheet in order, from the container that holds the least, to the container that holds the most. For each of the containers on the rest of the sheet, children tick to show whether they would measure the capacity using a cup or bucket.

© HarperCollins*Publishers* Ltd. 201

Name: _____ Date: _____

More than

Compare the capacity of containers

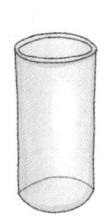     

Teacher's notes

Children look at each pair of containers and draw a circle around the container that holds more.

Name: _____ Date: _____

More, less or the same?

Compare capacities of containers with a litre

You will need:
- six containers of varying sizes
- litre jug
- water tray
- red and blue coloured pencils

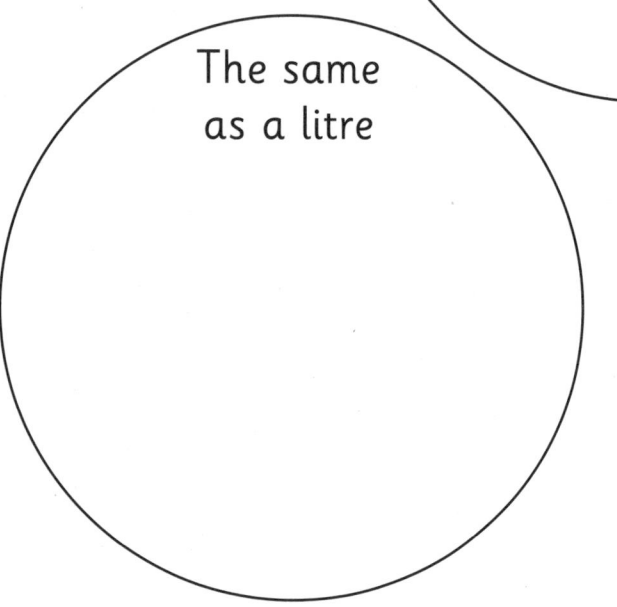

Less than a litre

The same as a litre

More than a litre

holds least   holds most

Teacher's notes

- Provide children with six containers labelled A–F (varied in size to match the labels in the circles). They estimate the capacity of the containers and decide whether the container holds 'less than', 'the same as' or 'more than' a litre and write the letter letter of the container inside one of the three circles using a red pencil.
- Then they use a litre jug to fill each container. They use a blue pencil to either tick the letter in the circle, if they estimated correctly, or to write the letter in the correct circle.
- Finally, children write the letters A–F in order of capacity, from the one that holds the least to the one that holds the most.

Name: _____ Date: _____

Number names to 20

Read and write numbers from 1 to 20 in numerals and words

11 ☐   15 ☐   19 ☐

12 ☐   16 ☐   20 ☐

13 ☐   17 ☐

14 ☐   18 ☐

Teacher's notes

Children cut out the sets from the bottom of the sheet. They then count the the number of buttons in each set and glue them next to the correct number.

fourteen    sixteen    eleven   eighteen    thirteen

seventeen    twelve    nineteen    fifteen 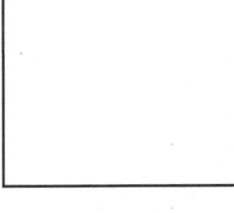   twenty

Name: _____ Date: _____

Tens and ones tents

Recognise place value in numbers beyond 20

You will need:
- scissors
- glue

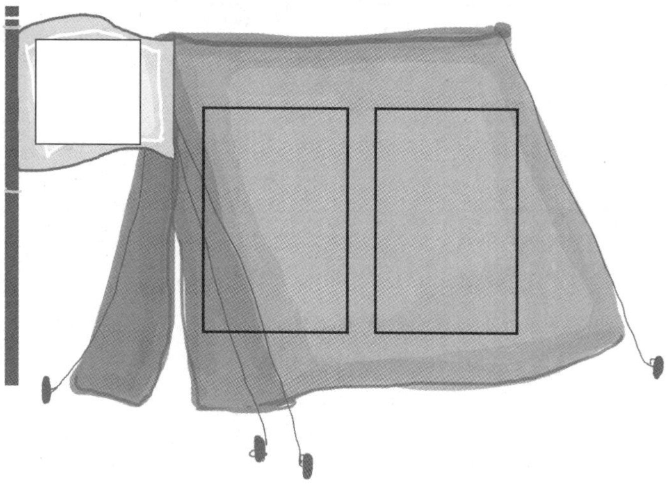

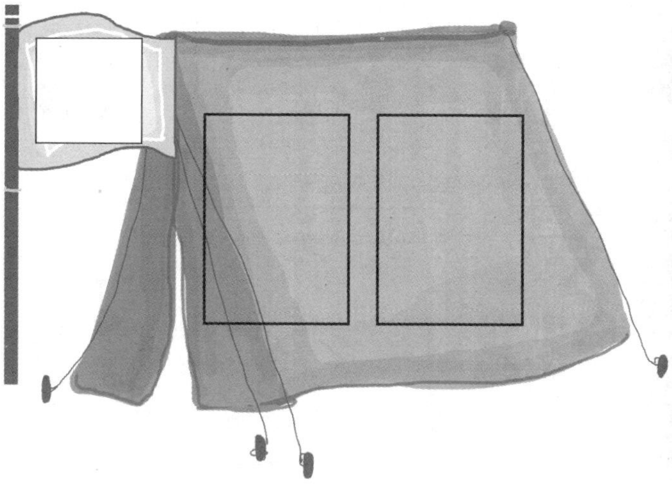

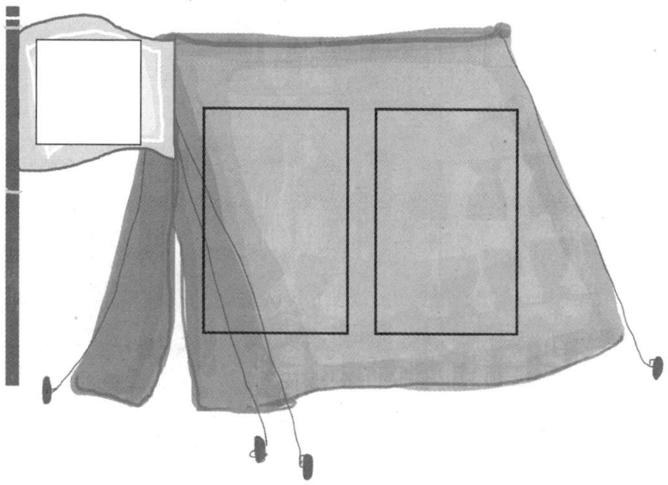

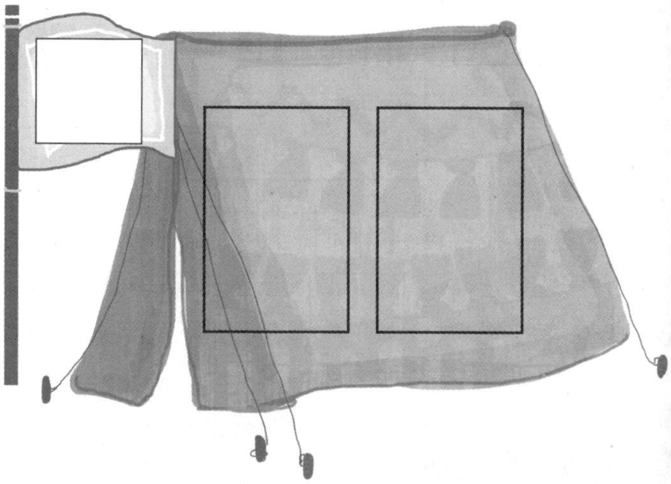

Teacher's notes

Children cut out the characters from the bottom of the sheet. They match each pair of characters by the patterns on their shirts and glue the matching pairs of characters on to a tent. They then write the two-digit number on the flag.

Name: _____ Date: _____

Cuckoo counting

Compare and order numbers to at least 30

You will need:
- yellow and green coloured pencils

Teacher's notes

For each set of three cuckoos, children colour the bird with the larger number in yellow and the bird with the smaller number in green. On the middle cuckoo, they write a number that lies between the two numbers.

Name: _____ Date: _____

Dinosaur tracks of 2

Count on in 2s

You will need:
- scissors
- glue

0 2 4 8 [ ] [ ]

1 3 [ ] 7 [ ] 11 [ ]

12 14 [ ] 18 20 [ ] [ ]

13 15 [ ] 19 21 [ ]

Teacher's notes

Children cut out the footprints from the bottom of the sheet. Then, in each sequence of footprints, count on in twos to find the missing numbers, and glue them in the in the appropriate pictures to complete each sequence.

23 25 12 16 24 13

6 9 22 10 5 17

Name: _____ Date: _____

Double decker doubles

Know doubles of all numbers from 1 to 10

You will need:
- scissors
- glue

10

16

12

18

14

20

Teacher's notes

Children cut out passengers from the bottom of the sheet. They then match each pair of passengers to the bus that shows their addition and glue them in.

5   9   8   7   9   6   10   7   5   6   8   10

Name: _____   Date: _____

Building block addition

Use doubles to solve addition problems

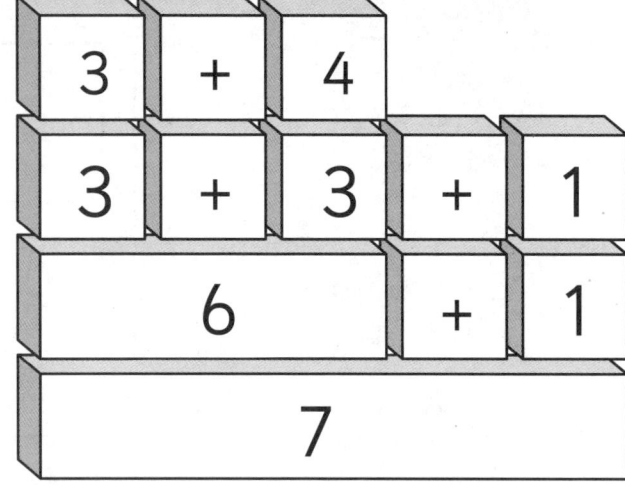

3 + 4

3 + 3 + 1

6 + 1

7

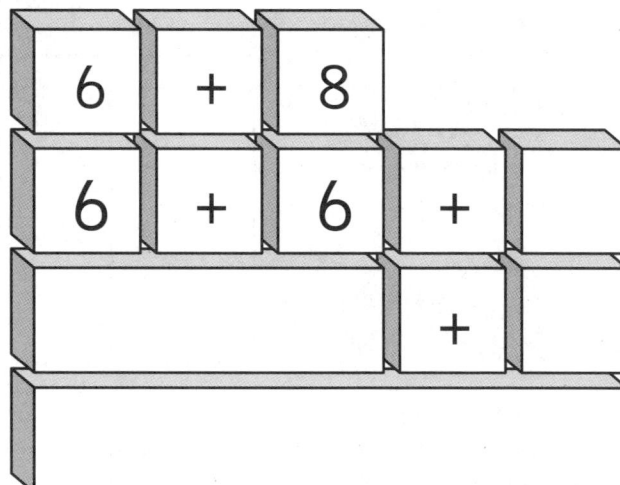

6 + 8

6 + 6 +

+

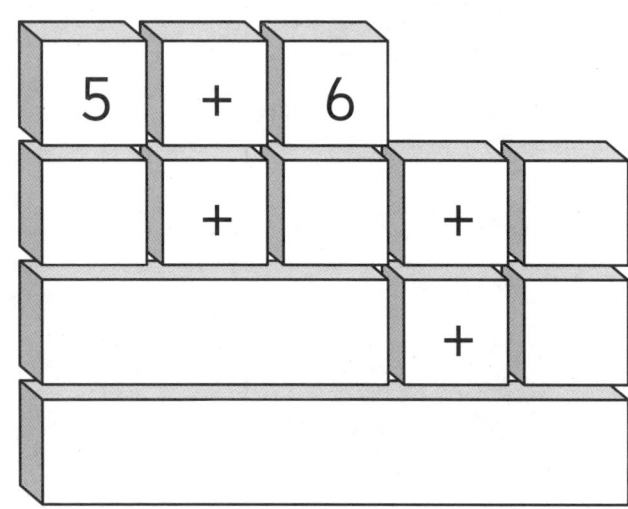

5 + 6

+ +

+

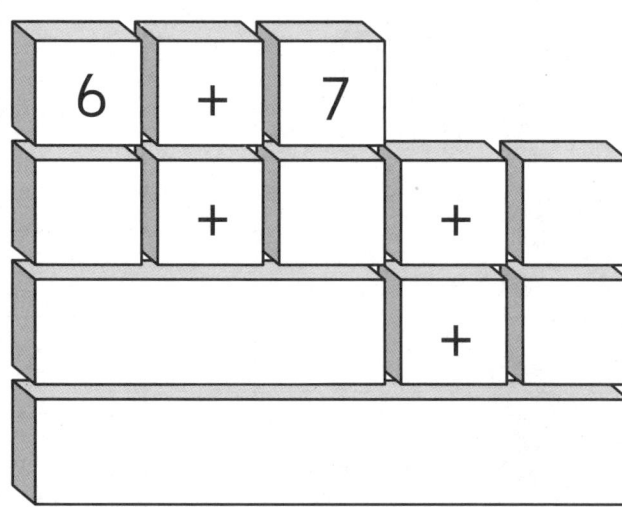

6 + 7

+ +

+

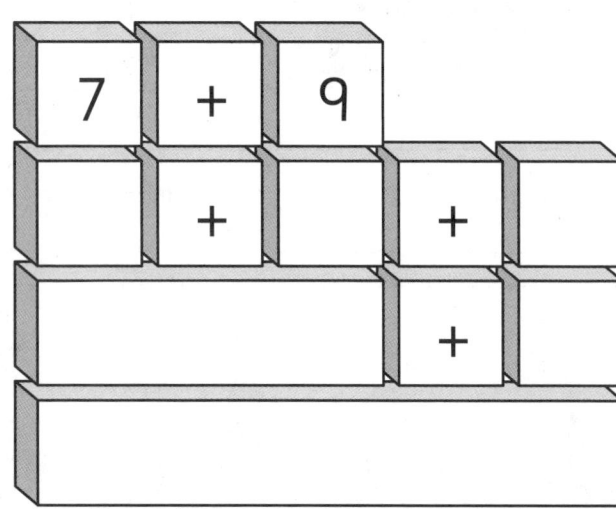

7 + 9

+ +

+

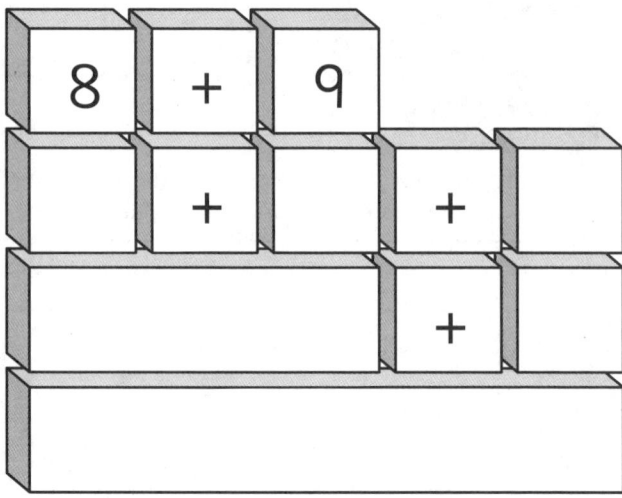

8 + 9

+ +

+

Name: _____ **Date:** _____

Tricky trios

Understand that addition can be done in any order

$$7 + 10 + 4 = 21$$

$$4 + 7 + 10 = \boxed{}$$

$$\boxed{} + \boxed{} + \boxed{} = \boxed{}$$

$$\boxed{} + \boxed{} + \boxed{} = \boxed{}$$

$$\boxed{} + \boxed{} + \boxed{} = \boxed{}$$

$$\boxed{} + \boxed{} + \boxed{} = \boxed{}$$

$$\boxed{} + \boxed{} + \boxed{} = \boxed{}$$

$$\boxed{} + \boxed{} + \boxed{} = \boxed{}$$

$$\boxed{} + \boxed{} + \boxed{} = \boxed{}$$

$$\boxed{} + \boxed{} + \boxed{} = \boxed{}$$

$$\boxed{} + \boxed{} + \boxed{} = \boxed{}$$

$$\boxed{} + \boxed{} + \boxed{} = \boxed{}$$

Teacher's notes

In each section, children look at the three numbers at the top and write them in the boxes of the first addition calculation. They work out the answer, then rearrange the numbers, twice, and complete each calculation by writing the answer.

Name: _____   Date: _____

Yellow submarines

You will need:
- scissors
- glue

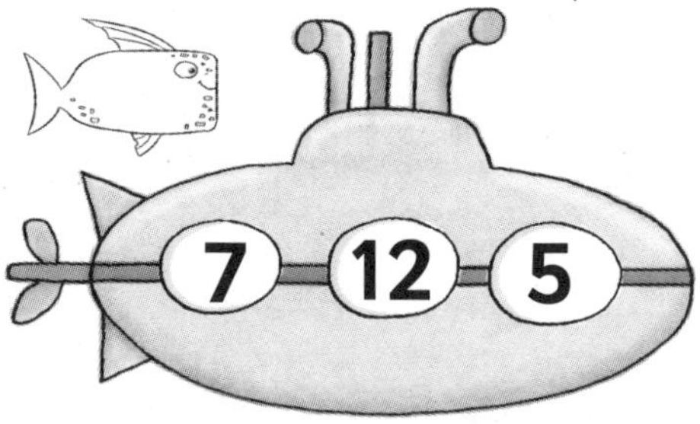

Recall addition and subtraction facts to 20, and use them to work out other facts

| 9 | 15 | 6 |

| 7 | 12 | 5 |

| 5 | 8 | 13 |

| 14 | 4 | 10 |

Teacher's notes

Children complete each addition and subtraction calculation at the bottom of the sheet. They then cut out each calculation, and glue one addition and one related subtraction fact to the submarine showing the same three numbers.

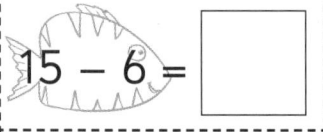

15 − 6 = ☐   10 + 4 = ☐   9 + 6 = ☐   14 − 4 = ☐

7 + 5 = ☐   12 − 7 = ☐   13 − 8 = ☐   8 + 5 = ☐

Name: _____ Date: _____

osition words

Understand position words

You will need:
- cardboard box
- small toy
- piece of paper
- cube
- ball
- book
- camera or coloured pencils

Teacher's notes

One at a time, read the following instructions to the children. The children should place each object in the described position.
- Put the cardboard box **on top of** the table.
- Put the toy **in front of** the cardboard box.
- Put the ball **inside** the cardboard box.
- Put the piece of paper **outside** the cardboard box on top of the table.
- Put the cube **underneath** the piece of paper.
- Put the book **behind** the cardboard box.

Once completed, children either draw the arrangement of the objects or, with adult support, take a photograph and glue it onto this sheet.

Name: _____ Date: _____

Farm positions

Understand position words

Name: _____ Date: _____

Directions

Understand and use direction words

Forward
Left ←→ Right
Backward

You will need:
• small toy person or building cube

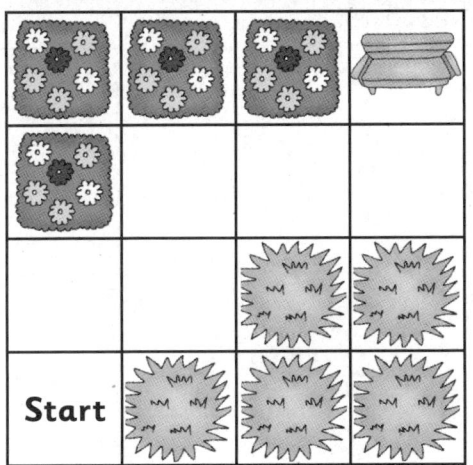

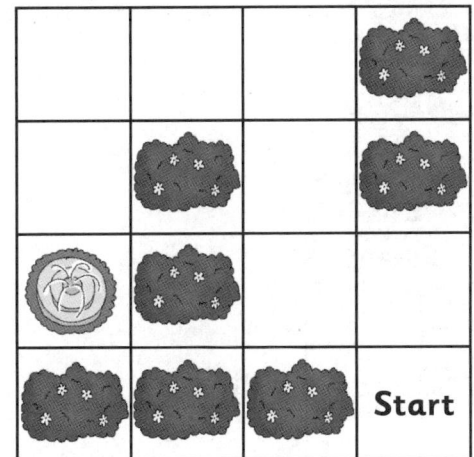

Forward ↑	Forward ↑	Forward ↑	
Left ←	Right →	Right →	
Forward ↑	Forward ↑	Forward ↑	
Forward ↑	Forward ↑	Right →	
Left ←	Right →	Right →	
Left ←	Right →	Forward ↑	
Backward ↓	Backward ↓		
Backward ↓	Backward ↓		
	Backward ↓		

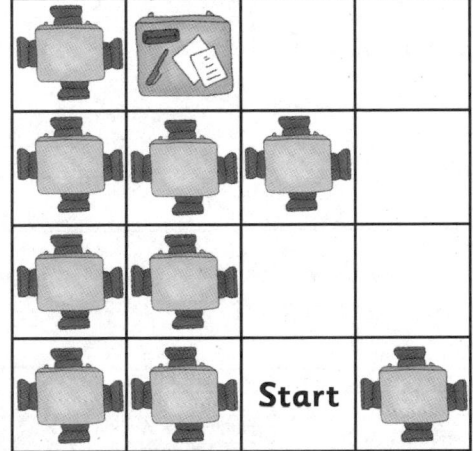

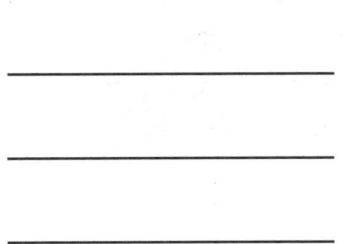

Teacher's notes

There are four grid routes, but only three complete sets of directions – one set of directions is missing. Children move a toy person or building cube along each grid route to match it to the correct set of directions. They draw a line a line to match each route to the correct set of directions. They then write the missing set of directions and draw a line to the grid route.

Name: _____ Date: _____

Turning

Recognise and make whole, half, quarter and three-quarter turns

You will need:
- scissors
- glue

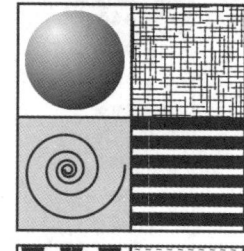 a quarter turn to the right

a half turn

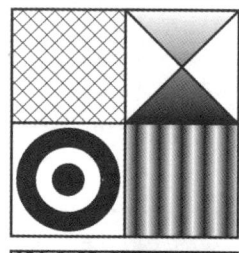 a quarter turn to the left

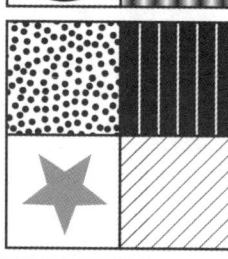 a three-quarter turn to the right

 a three-quarter turn to the left

Teacher's notes

Children cut out the patterns from the bottom of the sheet. They place each one on its matching pattern on the left and read the instructions. They then glue the pattern in the empty box to show its position after making the turn.

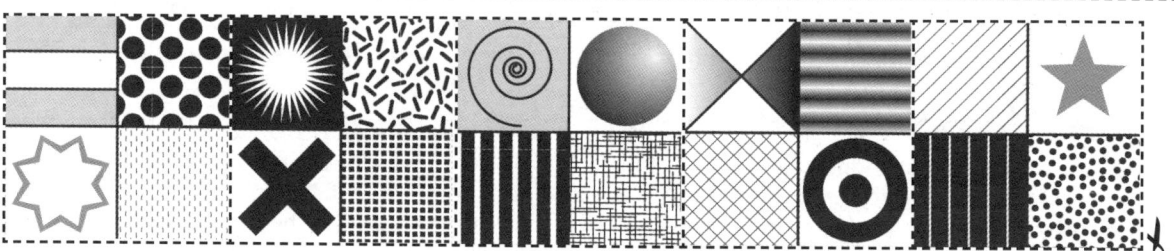

Name: _____ Date: _____

Ewe 2s
Count in 2s

8
6
4	2

2			

Count on

6
12
8	10

12			

Count back

20
18
16	14

14			

Count on

20	18
22
24

24			

Count back

30
26
24	28

24			

Count on

Teacher's notes

Children look at the sheep in each field, and use the four numbers to count on or back in twos. They write the numbers in the correct order in the spaces next to each field.

Name: _____ Date: _____

Pear pairs

Make connections between arrays,
number patterns and counting in 2s

You will need:
- scissors
- glue

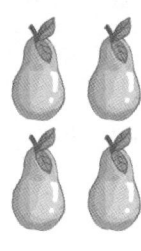

2 lots of 2 make ☐ .

3 lots of 2 make ☐ .

4 lots of 2 make ☐ .

5 lots of 2 make ☐ .

6 lots of 2 make ☐ .

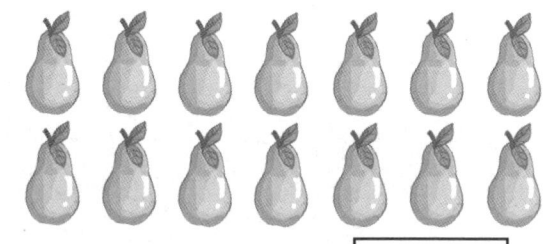

7 lots of 2 make ☐ .

Teacher's notes

Children cut out the multiples of 2 from the bottom of the sheet. They then look at each section and count in twos to find the total number of pears in each. Finally, they glue the corresponding number into the space next to the set of pears.

| 10 | 6 | 4 | 12 | 8 | 14 |

Name: _____ Date: _____

Hives and 10s

Count in 5s or 10s

15	**20**			
60	**70**			
35	**40**			
100	**90**			
50	**45**			

Name: _____ Date: _____

How many?

Make connections between arrays, number patterns and counting in 2s, 5s and 10s

You will need:
- scissors
- glue

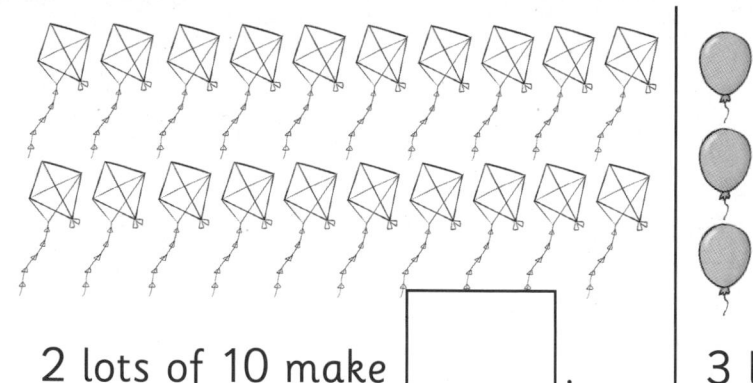

2 lots of 10 make ☐ .

3 lots of 5 make ☐ .

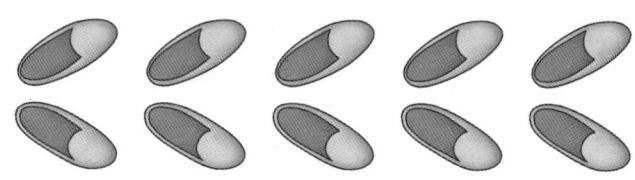

5 lots of 2 make ☐ .

4 lots of 10 make ☐ .

5 lots of 5 make ☐ .

7 lots of 2 make ☐ .

Teacher's notes

Children cut out the numbers from the bottom of the sheet. They then look at the instruction for each section, counting the objects in twos, fives or tens and glue the correct answer into each space.

| 40 | 15 | 14 | 20 | 25 | 10 |

Name: _____ **Date:** _____

low many sweets?

Count sets of 2, 5 or 10 to find a total

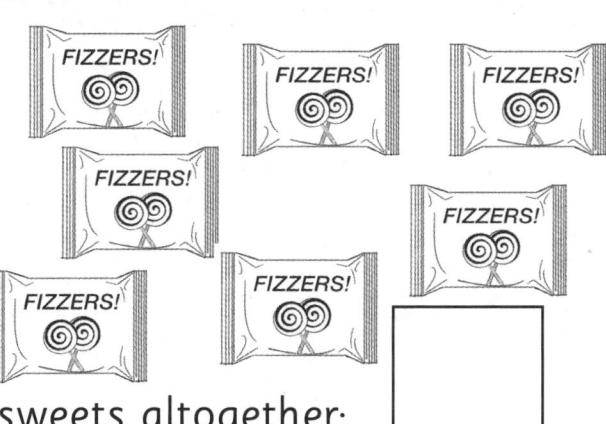

sweets altogether: ☐

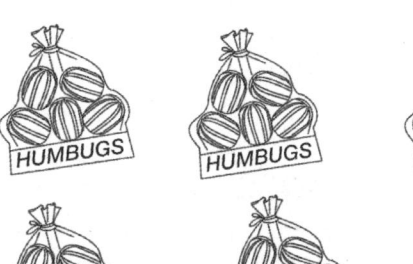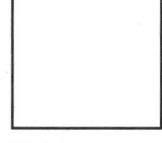

sweets altogether: ☐

sweets altogether: ☐

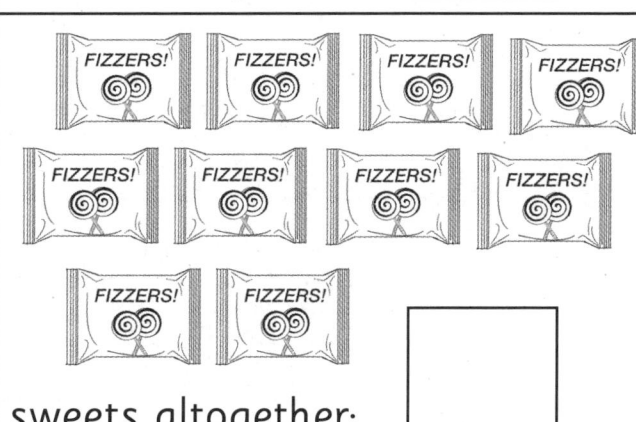

sweets altogether: ☐

sweets altogether: ☐

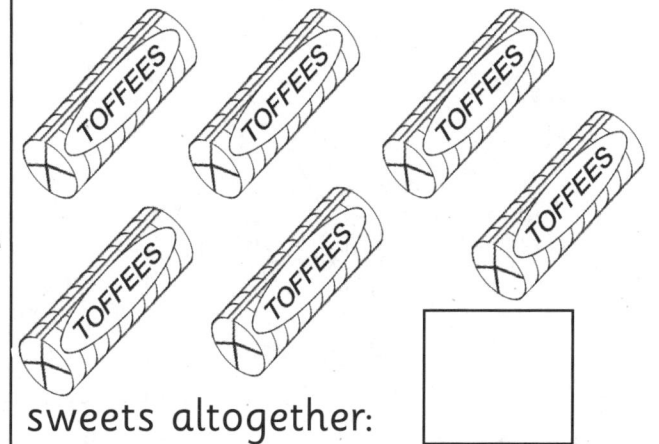

sweets altogether: ☐

| 25 | 60 | 40 | 14 | 20 | 45 |

Name: _____ Date: _____

Penny purses

Count sets of 2, 5 or 10 to find a total

You will need:
- scissors
- glue

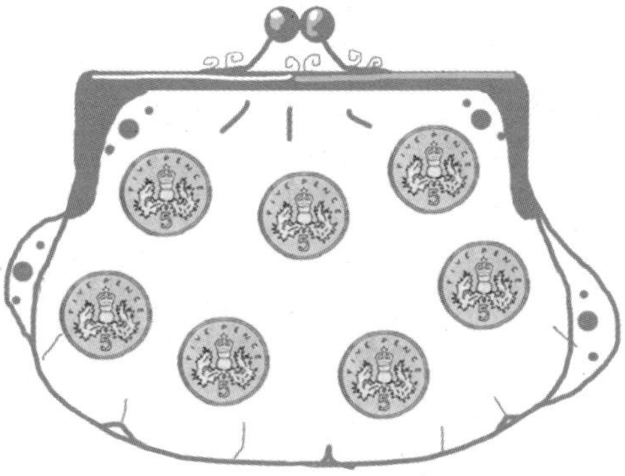

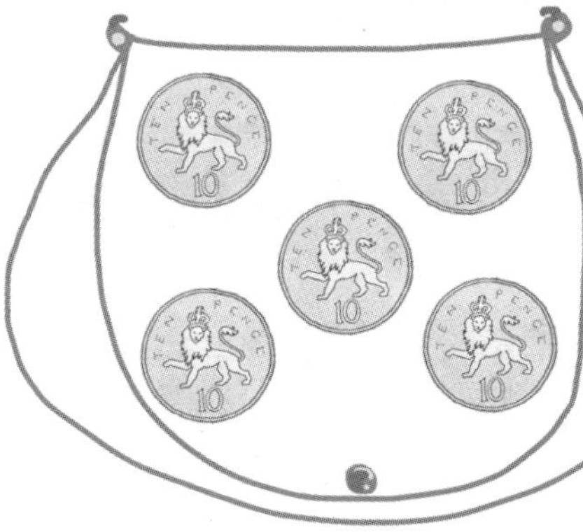

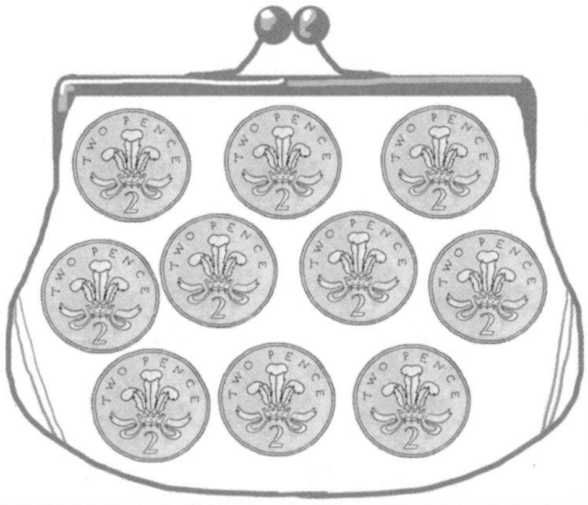

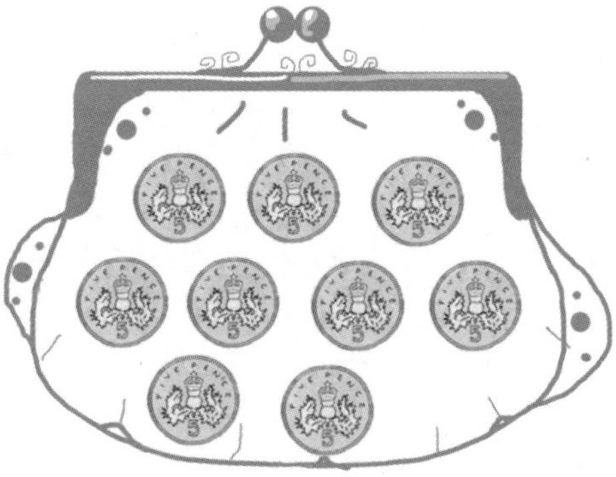

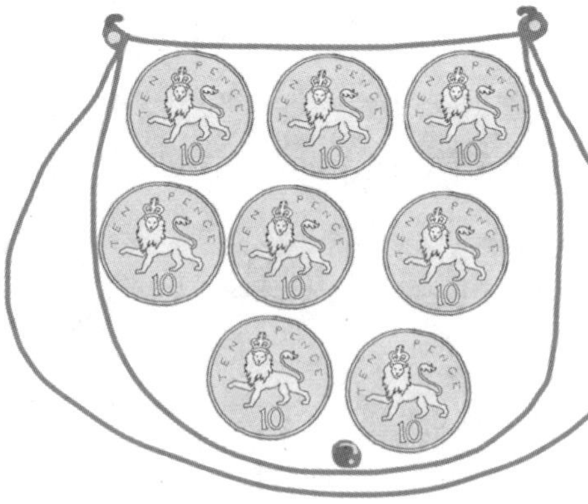

Teacher's notes

Children cut out the totals from the bottom of the sheet. They look at the 2p, 5p or 10p coins in each purse and work out the total amount in each one. Finally, they glue the correct total next to each purse.

| 50p | 45p | 14p | 20p | 35p | 80p |

Name: _____ Date: _____

Milkshake shares

Share objects into equal groups

☐ shared between:

is ☐ milkshakes each.

☐ shared between:

is ☐ milkshakes each.

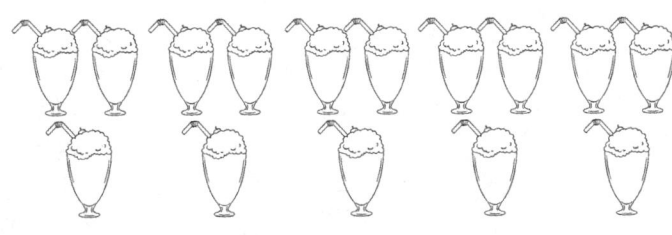

☐ shared between:

is ☐ milkshakes each.

☐ shared between:

is ☐ milkshakes each.

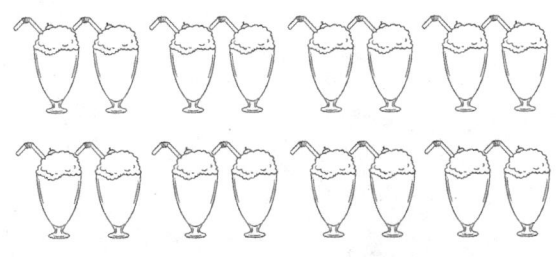

☐ shared between:

is ☐ milkshakes each.

☐ shared between:

is ☐ milkshakes each.

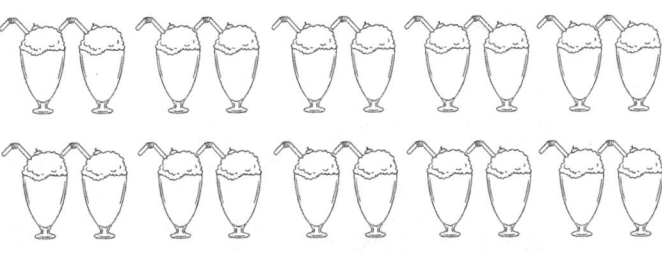

☐ shared between:

is ☐ milkshakes each.

☐ shared between:

is ☐ milkshakes each.

Teacher's notes

Children count each set of milkshakes and then share them equally between the first group of children. They then divide the same number of shakes between the second group of children.

Name: _____ Date: _____

Bird sharing

Share objects into equal groups

10 shared between **2** is ☐.

☐ shared between ☐ is ☐.

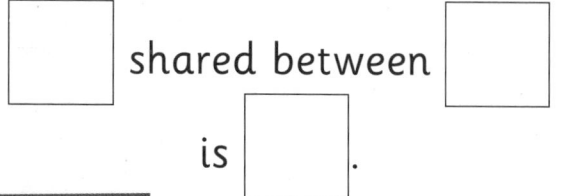

☐ shared between ☐ is ☐.

☐ shared between ☐ is ☐.

Name: _____ Date: _____

More or less than 1 metre?

Understand what a metre is

You will need:
- metre rule
- coloured pencils

Shorter than 1 metre	Longer/taller than 1 metre

Teacher's notes

- Children use a metre rule and compare the height or length of different items around the classroom to see whether they are shorter/longer/taller than a metre. They include at least three objects for each column. Finally, they draw pictures of each item.

Name: _____ Date: _____

Estimating and measuring

Estimate and measure lengths, widths and heights

You will need:
- ruler
- metre rule

Object	Estimate	Measurement
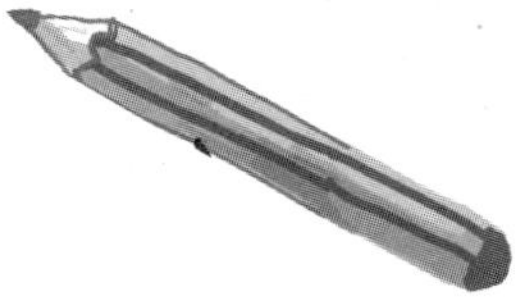		

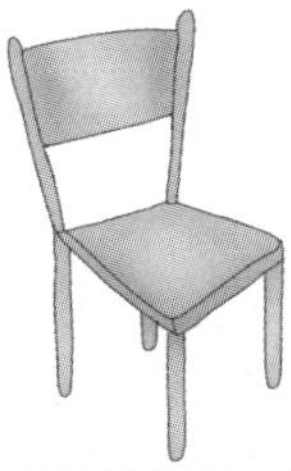		

Teacher's notes

Children estimate the length, width or height of each object and write down their estimate. They then measure the object using a ruler or metre rule and write the actual measurement.

Name: _____ Date: _____

low many bricks?

Solve problems about mass

3 bricks	6 bricks	2 bricks	8 bricks

The book  is ⬜ bricks heavier than the teddy  .

The pencil  is ⬜ bricks lighter than the book  .

Teacher's notes

Children work out the different weight combinations of each pair of items on one side of the balance. They then write the number of bricks that are needed to make it balance. Finally, they complete the questions.

Name: _____ Date: _____

Shapes that balance

Solve problems about mass

You will need:
- scissors
- glue
- paper
- balance
- interlocking cubes

Teacher's notes

Children cut out the shapes. They count the cubes to find the shapes that would balance and stick them next to each other on another piece of paper. They then make the shapes and check their answers using a real balance.

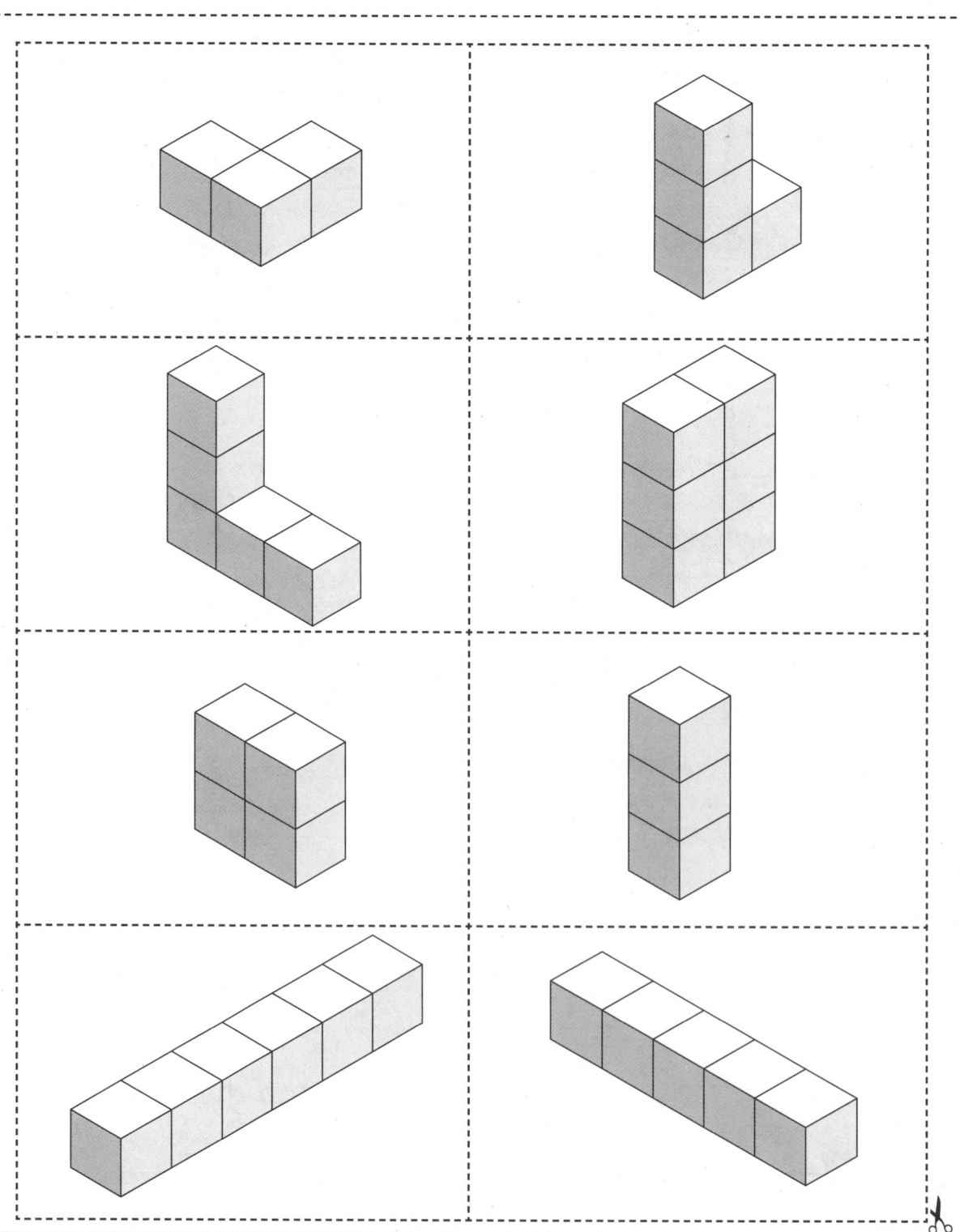

Name: _____ Date: _____

Monkey-puzzle trees

Know addition and subtraction facts to 20

[ ] (+) [ ] (=) [ ]

[ ] (−) [ ] (=) [ ]

[ ] ( ) [ ] ( ) [ ]

[ ] ( ) [ ] ( ) [ ]

[ ] ( ) [ ] ( ) [ ]

[ ] ( ) [ ] ( ) [ ]

Teacher's notes

Children count the total number of monkeys in the two trees and complete the addition calculation underneath. They then complete the subtraction calculations by counting the number of monkeys in the tree, and then subtracting those that have been crossed out.

Name: _____ Date: _____

Magic carpet calculations

Recognise patterns in addition and subtraction facts

19 + 0 = ▢

18 + ▢ = 19

17 + ▢ = 19

▢ + ▢ = 19

19 – 0 = ▢

19 – 1 = ▢

▢ – 2 = 17

▢ – ▢ = ▢

20 – 4 = ▢

20 – 5 = ▢

▢ – 6 = ▢

▢ – ▢ = ▢

20 + 0 = ▢

19 + ▢ = 20

18 + ▢ = 20

▢ + ▢ = 20

Teacher's notes

Children look at each set of addition and subtraction calculations and continue the pattern on each of the magic carpets, writing the correct numbers into the spaces.

Name: _____ Date: _____

Seaside problems (1)

Solve word problems

We got the train at 9 o'clock. It took 2 hours to get there.

We got there at ☐ o'clock.

Lee found 13 shells on the beach but she dropped 3.

She still had ☐ shells.

Amir brought 6 pasties with him.

Naomi brought 6 too!

They had ☐ altogether.

We had 12 tickets for the fair rides.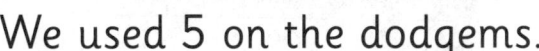

We used 5 on the dodgems.

We had ☐ tickets left.

Teacher's notes

Children cut out the addition and subtraction calculations from the bottom of the sheet. They read each word problem and then decide which calculation belongs with each one before completing the calculation and gluing it into place. Finally, they complete each sentence underneath.

12 – 5 = ☐   9 + 2 = ☐   13 – 3 = ☐   6 + 6 = ☐

Name: _____ Date: _____

Seaside problems (2)

Solve word problems

Samir finds 11 shells.
He drops 3.

☐ ◯ ☐ ◯ ☐

Then Ella gives him 5 more.

☐ ◯ ☐ ◯ ☐

Now Samir has ☐ shells.

The children have 15 sandwiches.
A bird takes 2.

☐ ◯ ☐ ◯ ☐

They eat 4.

☐ ◯ ☐ ◯ ☐

There are ☐ sandwiches left.

The children make 18 sandcastles
but the sea washes 5 away.

☐ ◯ ☐ ◯ ☐

They make 7 more.

☐ ◯ ☐ ◯ ☐

They have ☐ sandcastles
altogether.

Ayesha and
Finn counted
12 fish in the
rock pool.

Then 4 more swam in.

☐ ◯ ☐ ◯ ☐

Then 10 swam away.

☐ ◯ ☐ ◯ ☐

There were ☐ fish left.

Teacher's notes

Children read each word problem and then write the addition or subtraction calculations in the spaces provided.
They then write their own addition and subtraction problems on the back of the sheet using these numbers as the
answers: 10, 15, 7 and 20.

Name: _____ Date: _____

Penny problems

Know addition and subtraction facts to 20

Ellia has 20p. She buys a balloon. How much does she have left?

9p

⬜ ⭕ ⬜ ⭕ ⬜

Show her change.

Joe buys a card and a pen.

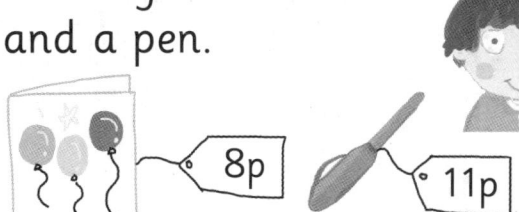

8p   11p

How much does he spend?

⬜ ⭕ ⬜ ⭕ ⬜

Show his total.

Maya buys a notebook and a pencil. How much does she spend?

Notebook 13p   7p

⬜ ⭕ ⬜ ⭕ ⬜

Show her total.

Leon has 20p. He buys a dinosaur.

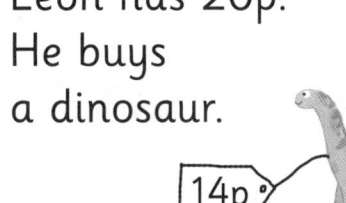

14p

How much does he have left?

⬜ ⭕ ⬜ ⭕ ⬜

Show his change.

Teacher's notes

Children complete each money problem, reading each one carefully to decide whether it is an addition or a subtraction calculation. They then draw a ring around the coins to show each character's change or total amount spent.

Name: _____ Date: _____

Pizza toppings

Solve problems involving money

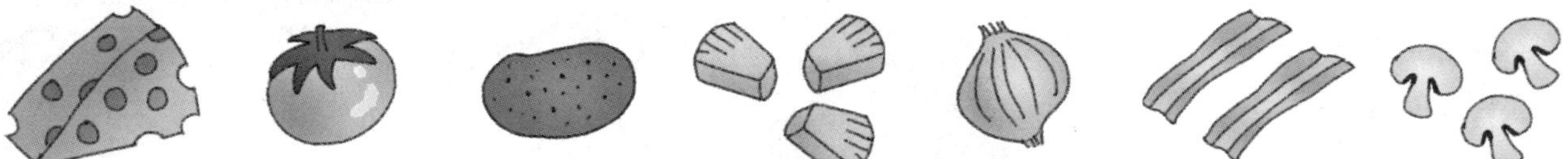

6p   8p   12p   9p   5p   13p   7p

Megan   [ ] p ◯ [ ] p ◯ [ ] p

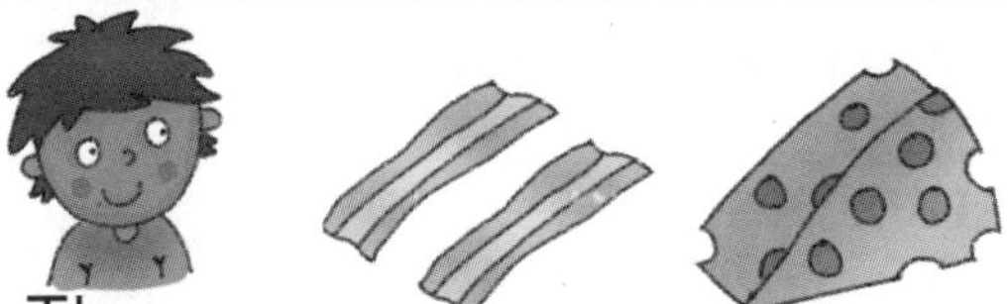

Theo   [ ] p ◯ [ ] p ◯ [ ] p

Elise   [ ] p ◯ [ ] p ◯ [ ] p

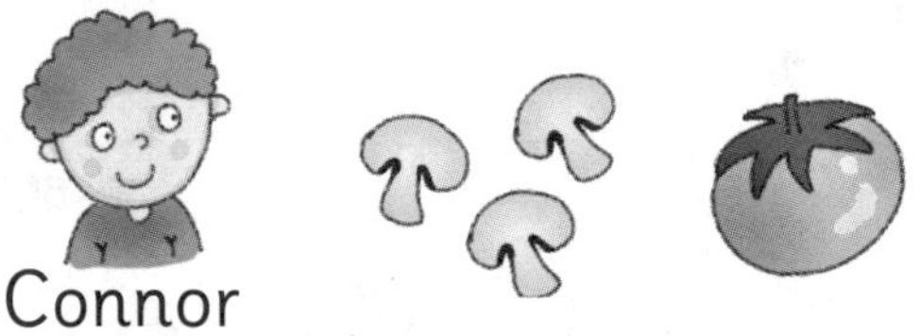

Connor   [ ] p ◯ [ ] p ◯ [ ] p

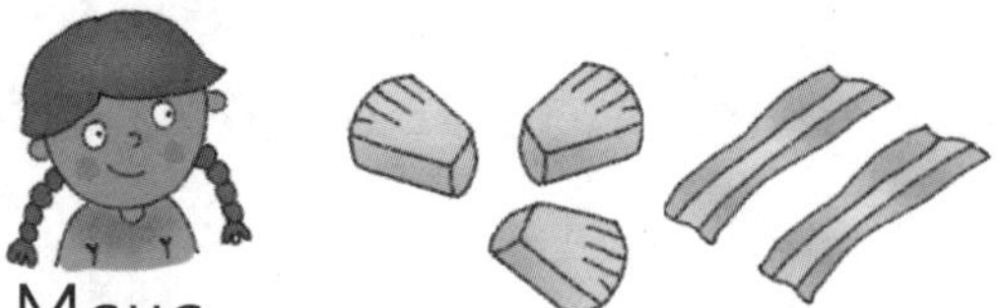

Maya   [ ] p ◯ [ ] p ◯ [ ] p

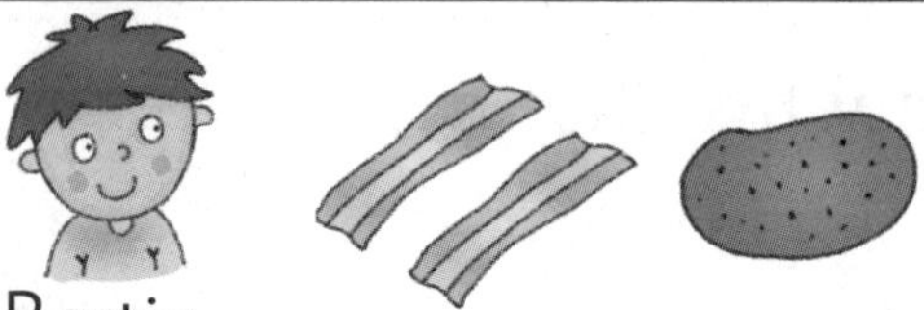

Bertie   [ ] p ◯ [ ] p ◯ [ ] p

Everyone has 20p to spend on pizza toppings. Can you work out their change?

Teacher's notes

Children work out the cost of the pizza toppings for each person, then answer the question at the bottom, writing their answers on the back of this sheet.

Name: _____ Date: _____

Tremendous trios

Recognise and find related addition and subtraction facts

6	+	9	=	15
9	+	6	=	
15	−		=	
15	−		=	

11	+	5	=	
	+		=	
	−		=	
	−		=	

9	+	8	=	
	+		=	
	−		=	
	−		=	

Teacher's notes

Children use the numbers in each trio to complete the related addition and subtraction facts. There are two addition facts and two subtraction facts for each trio.

Name: _____ Date: _____

10 more or less town

Add and subtract 10 to or from a number

13   17   19   21   25   26   30   34

20

27

11

3

44

29

16

35

Teacher's notes

Children look at the number on each child's t-shirt, and match each one to the house that shows ten more or ten less than their number. Children then find 10 more and 10 less than each of these numbers: 10, 15, 23, 29, 37 and 41, writing the answers on the back of this sheet.

Name: _____ Date: _____

2-D shape patterns

Complete 2-D shape patterns

Key:
red = 1
yellow = 2
green = 3
blue = 4
purple = 5

You will need:
- ruler
- red, yellow, green, blue and purple coloured pencils

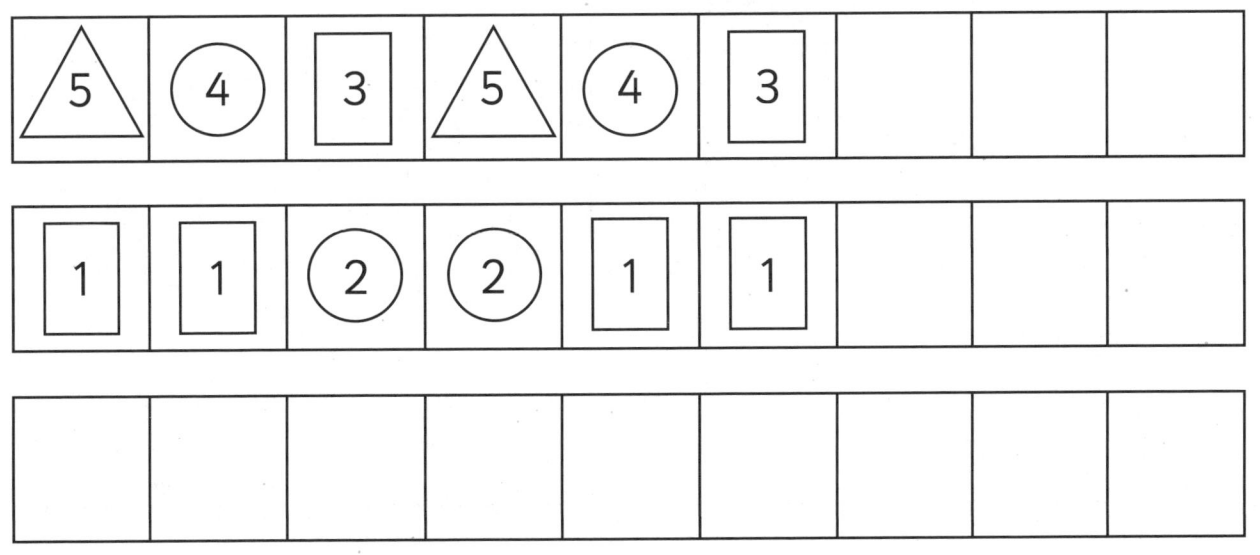

| 5 | 4 | 3 | 5 | 4 | 3 | | | |

| 1 | 1 | 2 | 2 | 1 | 1 | | | |

| | | | | | | | | |

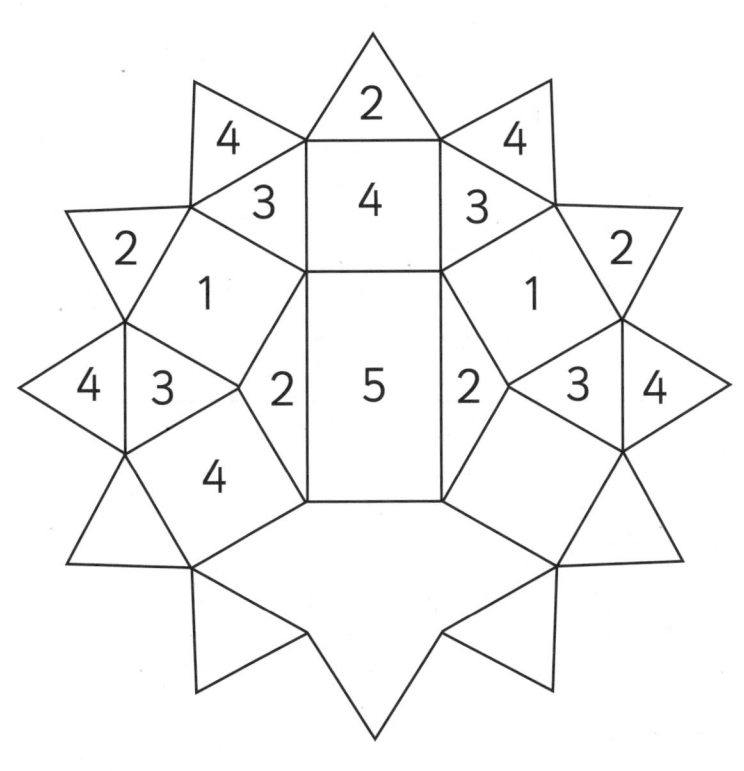

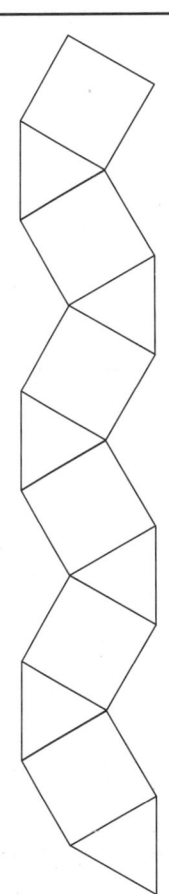

Name: ______________________ Date: ____________

Drawing 2-D shapes

Recognise and draw 2-D shapes

You will need:
- coloured pencils

rectangle circle triangle square

____

____

____

____

____

____

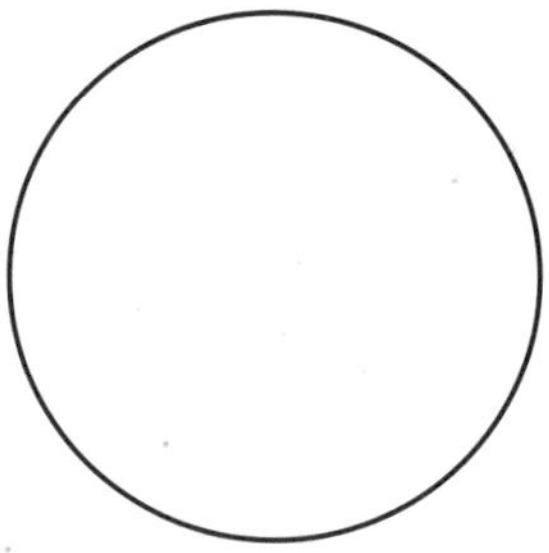

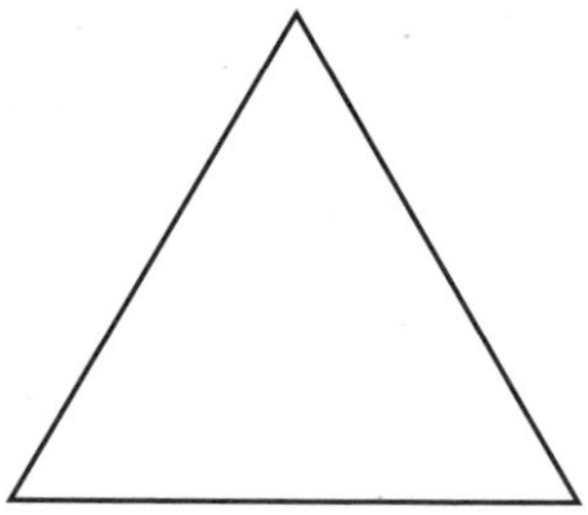

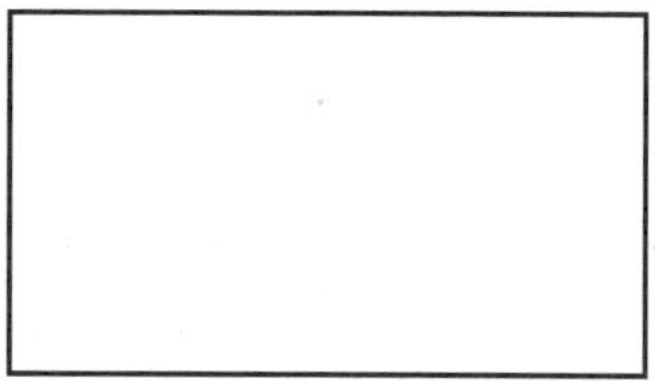

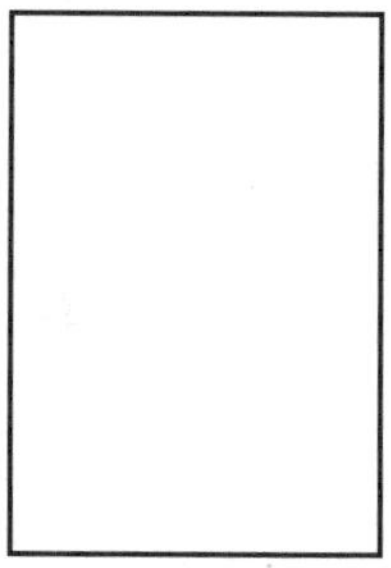

Teacher's notes

For each of the five shapes shown, children write the name of each shape underneath. Then beside each of the shapes they draw a picture of a real-life object that is the same shape. For example, they might draw a clock face for a circle. Finally, in the bottom right, they draw and name their own shape and then draw a picture of a real-life object that is the same shape.

Name: _____ Date: _____

-D shape patterns and models

Make patterns and models using 3-D shapes

You will need:
- 3-D shapes
  (spheres, cylinders,
  cones, cuboids,
  cubes, pyramids)
- coloured pencils or
  camera

My two-shape pattern:

My three-shape pattern:

My model:

Teacher's notes

Children use the 3-D shapes to create a two-shape repeating pattern (e.g. a, b, a, b, …) and a three-shape repeating pattern (e.g. a, b, c, a, b, c, …). They then make a model of a castle, train or similar using at least one of each of the six 3-D shapes. Children either draw their patterns and model or, with adult support, take a photograph of each and glue them onto this sheet.

Name: _____ Date: _____

3-D shape match

Recognise 3-D shapes in real life

You will need:
• coloured pencils

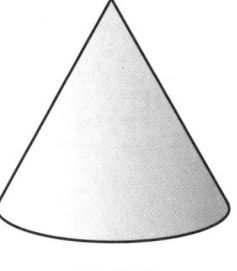

cone

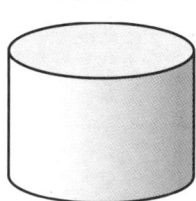

cylinder

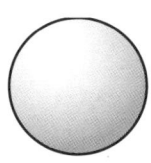

sphere

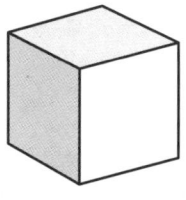

cube

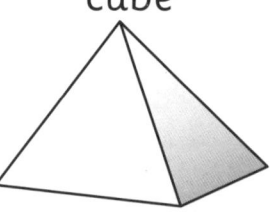

pyramid

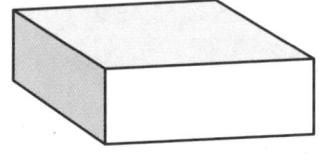

cuboid

Teacher's notes

Children draw a line from each object to the matching 3-D shape. They then decorate and colour the 3-D shapes to look like the objects.

Name: _____ Date: _____

Treasure doubles

Double numbers and sets

 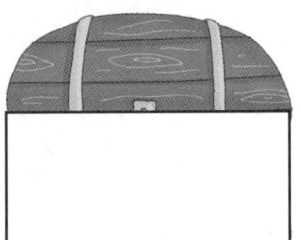

Double 5 is [ ] .

 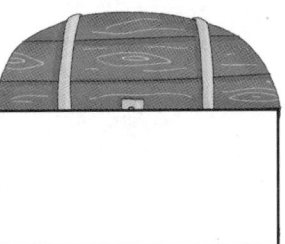

Double 8 is [ ] .

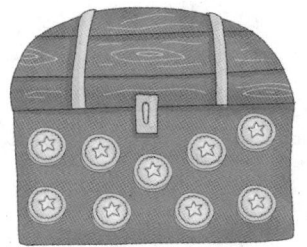 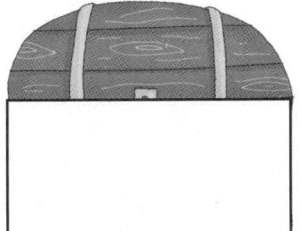

Double 9 is [ ] .

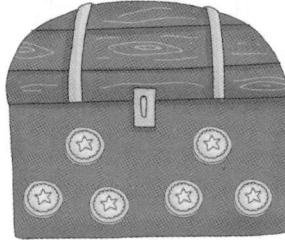 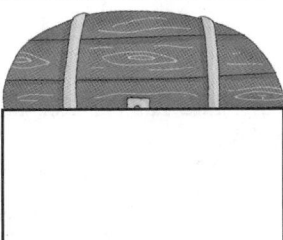

Double 6 is [ ] .

 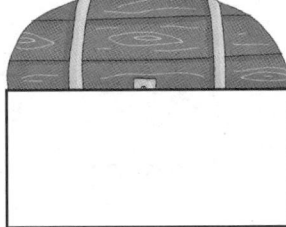

Double 7 is [ ] .

 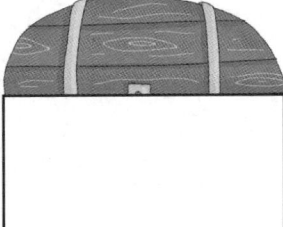

Double 10 is [ ] .

Teacher's notes

- Children cut out the sets of coins from the bottom of the sheet. They match each one to the treasure chest showing the same number to find the double, then complete each sentence underneath.

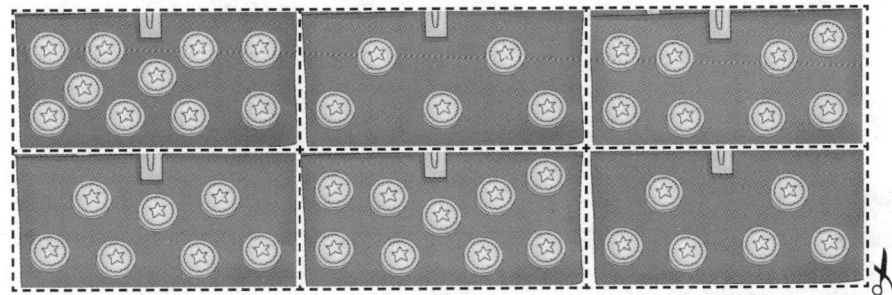

Name: _____ Date: _____

Spotted hanky halves

You will need:
• coloured pencils

Find half of a number or set of objects

Half of [ ] is [ ] .

Half of [ ] is [ ] .

Half of [ ] is [ ] .

Half of [ ] is [ ] .

Half of [ ] is [ ] .

Half of [ ] is [ ] .

Teacher's notes

Children count the total number of spots on each hanky and then colour half of them. They then complete the sentence underneath each one.

Name: _____ Date: _____

Fraction flags

Find one quarter of a number or set of objects

You will need:
• scissors
• glue
• coloured pencils

Children cut out thee labels from the bottom of the sheet. They count the spots, stars or diamonds on each flag and match the label that shows its total, then glue it in place. Finally, they colour one quarter of each of the patterns, and complete each sentence to show this number.

One quarter of 16 is ☐ . $\frac{1}{4}$ of 12 is ☐ .

$\frac{1}{4}$ of 24 is ☐ .   One quarter of 20 is ☐ .

Name: _____ Date: _____

Half and quarter constellations

Find doubles, halves and quarters of numbers

You will need:
- scissors
- glue
- yellow coloured pencil

Teacher's notes

Children cut out the labels from the bottom of the sheet. They count the total number of stars in each group to find which label should be glued underneath. Finally, they work out each calculation and colour the correct number of stars to show the answer.

$\frac{1}{2}$ of 10	$\frac{1}{4}$ of 12	$\frac{1}{4}$ of 20
half of 14	quarter of 8	$\frac{1}{2}$ of 18

Name: _____ Date: _____

Finding fractions

Find one half and one quarter of a shape

You will need:
- scissors
- glue
- coloured pencils

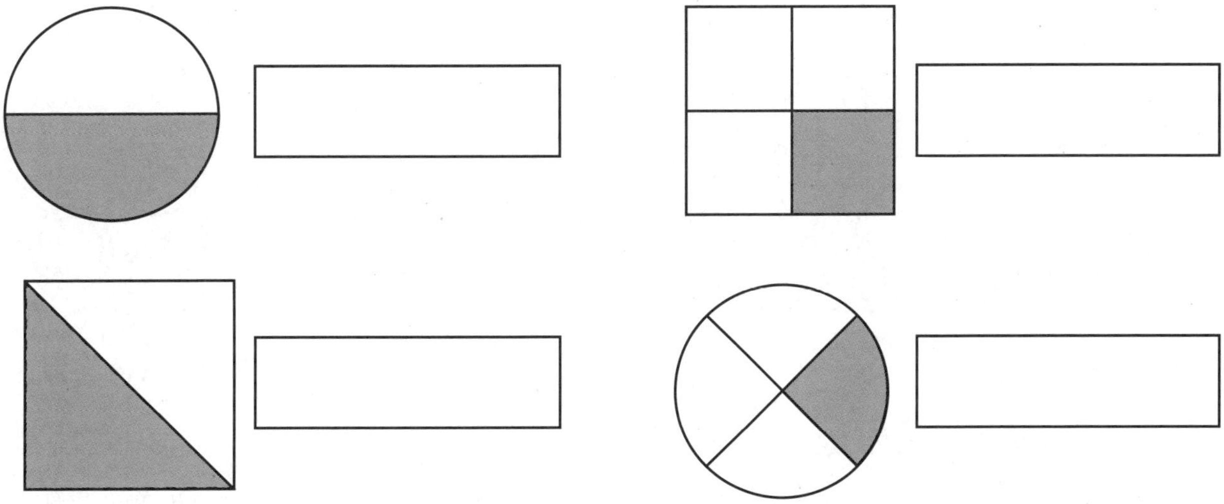

Colour one half of each shape.

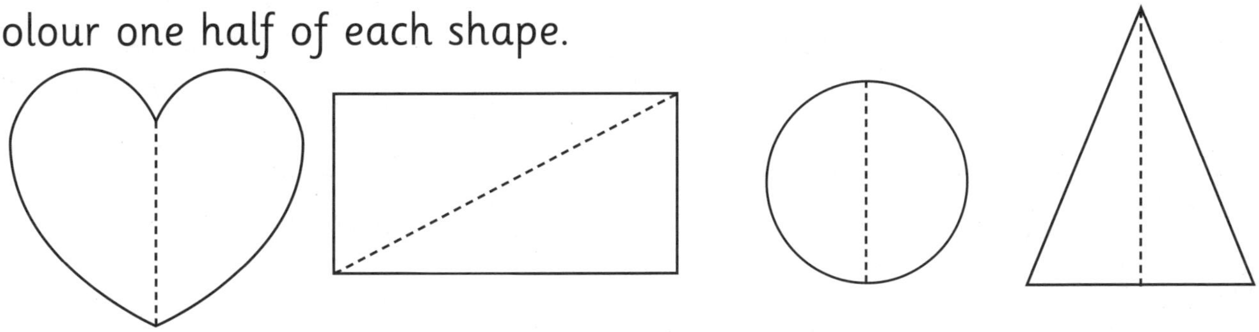

Colour one quarter of each shape.

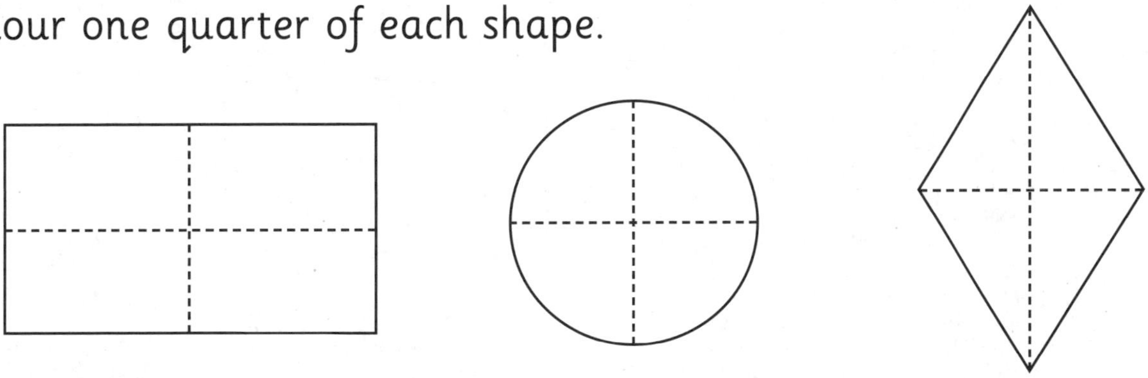

Teacher's notes

At the top of the page, children cut out the labels from the bottom of the sheet and match them to the shapes according to the fraction that is shaded. At the bottom of the page, they then divide and colour one half or one quarter of each shape.

| $\frac{1}{2}$ | one half | one quarter | $\frac{1}{4}$ |

Name: _____ Date: _____

Button halves and quarters

Find one half or one quarter of a set of objects

You will need:
• coloured pencils

Colour one half.

$\frac{1}{2}$ of ⬚ is ⬚ .

Colour one quarter.

$\frac{1}{4}$ of ⬚ is ⬚ .

Colour one half.

$\frac{1}{2}$ of ⬚ is ⬚ .

Colour one quarter.

$\frac{1}{4}$ of ⬚ is ⬚ .

Teacher's notes

Children count the number of buttons in each set, and colour one half or one quarter of the set as indicated. They then complete the sentences underneath.

Name: _____ Date: _____

our flag fractions

Understand that two halves make one whole

You will need:
- coloured pencils

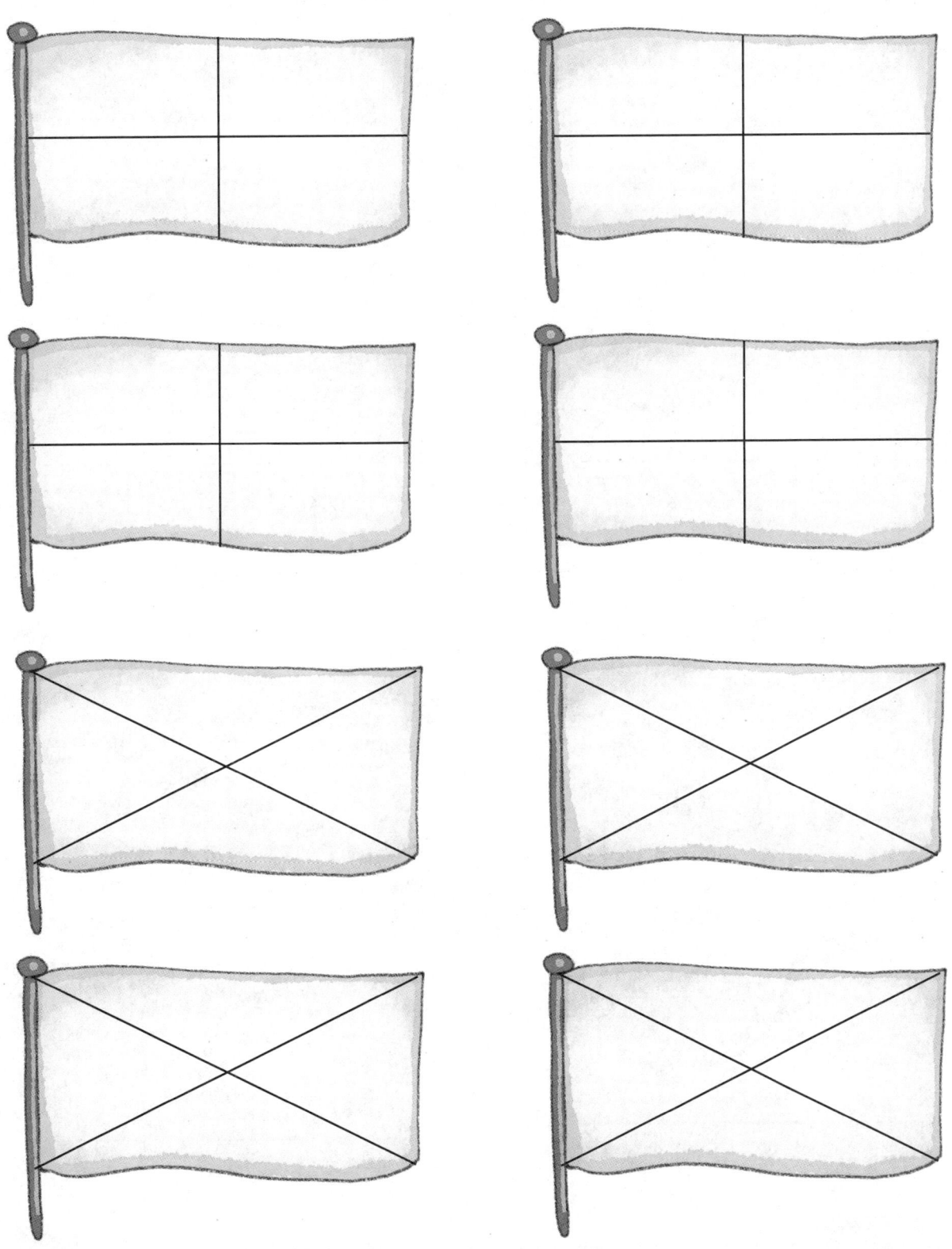

Children find as many different ways as possible to colour half of each flag, using one colour per flag.

Name: _____ Date: _____

Collect the marbles!

Understand that fractions are related to grouping and sharing

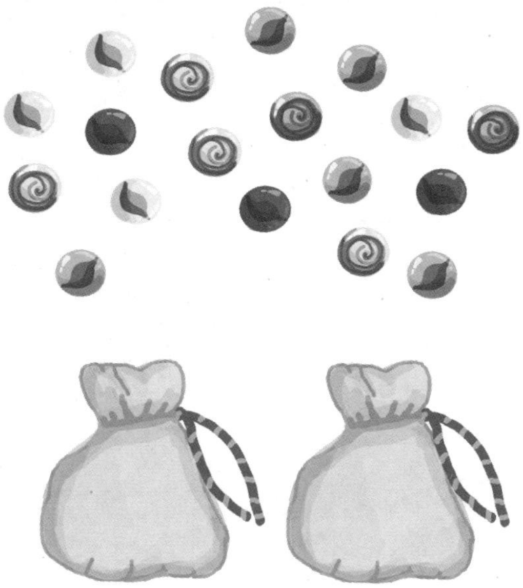

| | of | | is | | . | | | of | | is | | . |

| | of | | is | | . | | | of | | is | | . |

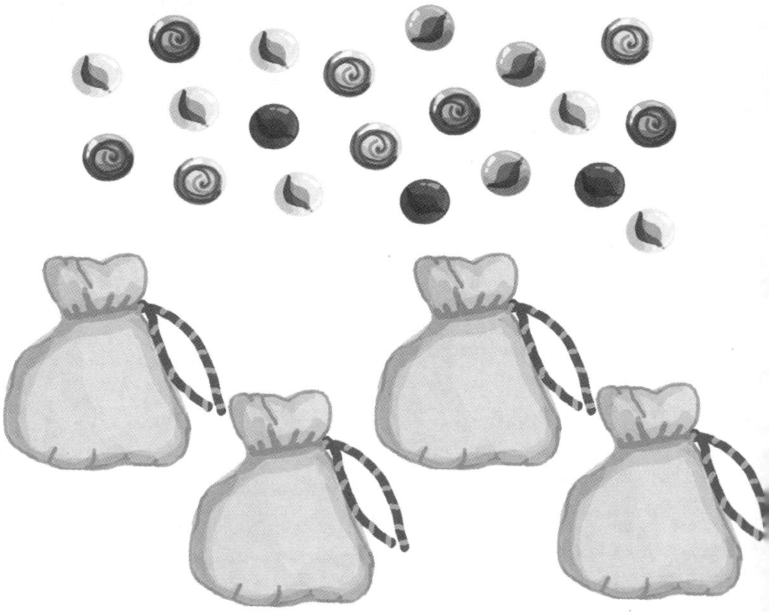

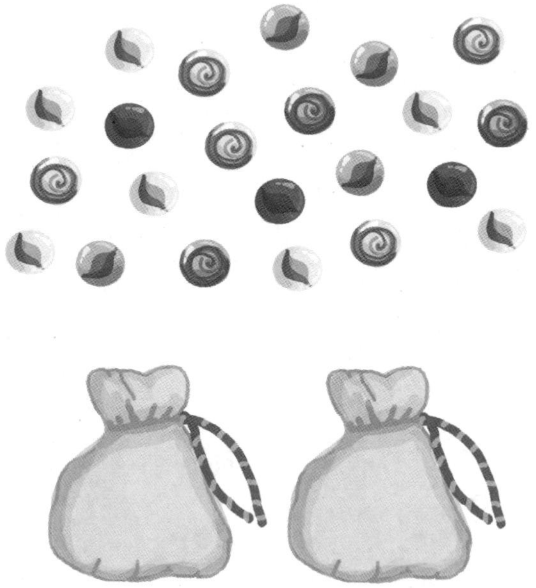

Teacher's notes

Children count the marbles in each set and by drawing marbles in the bags, share them into halves or quarters depending on the number of marble bags in the section. They then complete each sentence underneath to show one half or one quarter of each number.

Name: _____ Date: _____

My day

Read times on clocks and understand time intervals

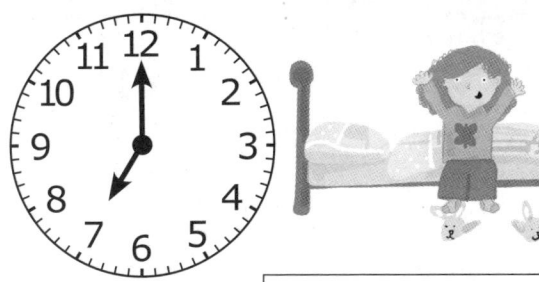

The time is [   ] .

Half an hour later the time is:  [   ] .

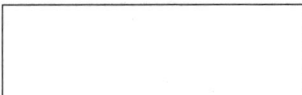

The time is [   ] .

One hour later the time is: [   ] .

The time is [   ] .

One hour earlier the time is: [   ] .

The time is [   ] .

Half an hour earlier the time is: [   ] .

Teacher's notes

Children look at the first clock in each row and write the time in the box underneath. They then read the second clock and sentence, and complete the sentence by writing the correct time in the box.

Name: ______________________ Date: ______________

Drawing hands

Read and draw hands on clocks to show the time to the hour and half hour

 1 hour earlier ←  → 1 hour later 

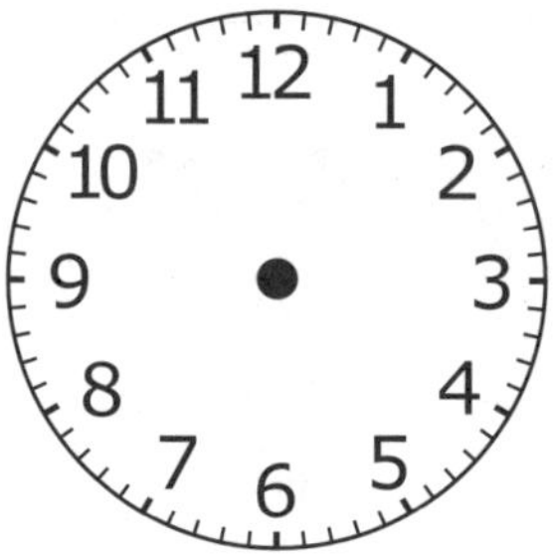 ½ hour earlier ←  → 1 hour later 

 1 hour earlier ←  → ½ hour later 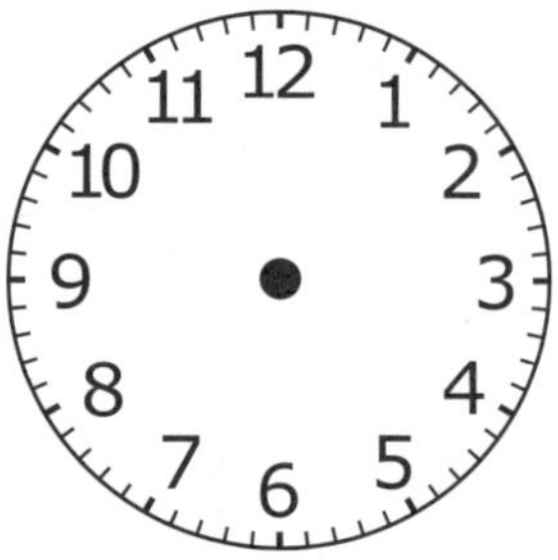

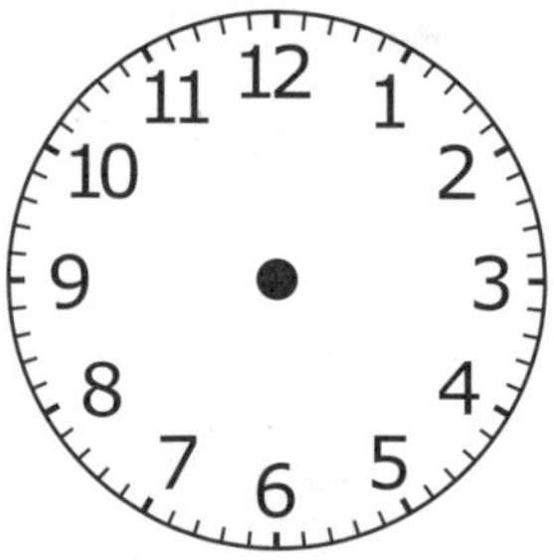 1 hour earlier ←  → 2 hours later 

 2 hours earlier ←  → 1 hour later 

Teacher's notes

For each row of clocks children read the time on the middle clock then draw hands on the other two clock faces to show the earlier and later times as shown on the arrows.

Name: _____ Date: _____

Things I can do in 1 minute

Begin to understand how long 1 minute is

You will need:
- 1-minute sand timer
- blocks
- beads and string
- counters
- paper

Number of times
I can write my
name:

Number
of hops
I can do:

Number
I can
count to:

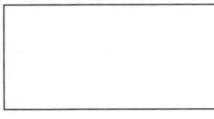

Number of blocks
I can build into
a tower:

Number of beads
I can thread
on a string:

Number of counters
I can put in
a long line:

Teacher's notes

Children perform each activity and record how many of each thing can be done in one minute.

Name: _____ Date: _____

Train times

Solve problems relating to time

Train A	Train B	Train A arrived at the station

_____ _____

Train A arrived at the station

_____

_____

than Train B.

_____

Train A	Train B	Train A arrived at the station

_____ _____

Train A arrived at the station

_____

_____

than Train B.

_____

Train A	Train B	Train A arrived at the station

_____ _____

Train A arrived at the station

_____

_____

than Train B.

Teacher's notes

For each pair of clocks children read the arrival time for Train A and Train B, and write the time underneath. They then read each sentence writing down how much earlier or later Train A arrived at the station compared to Train B.